Reboot
Your
Marriage

7 Way To Dump The Junk

Wesley & Neesha
Stringfellow

Unless otherwise indicated, all scripture quotations, references and definitions are from the Authorized King James Version © 1987; The New King James Version © 1982 by Thomas Nelson, Inc.; The New International Version 1973, 1978, 1984 by International Bible Society by the Zondervan Corporation; The Amplified Bible Old Testament © 1962, 1964, 1965, 1987 by the Zondervan Corporation; The Amplified New Testament © 1954, 1958, 1987 by the Lockman Foundation; The Message. Copyright © 1993, 1994, 1995, 1996, 2000, 2001, 2002. Used by permission of NavPress Publishing Group. All rights reserved; M.G. Easton M.A., D.D., Illustrated Bible Dictionary, Third Edition, published by Thomas Nelson, 1897; The Name Book © 1982, 1997 by Dorothy Astoria.

REBOOT YOUR MARRIAGE
7 Ways To Dump The Junk

Themarriagereboot.com
(708) 480-2907

Wesley & Neesha Stringfellow
Post Office Box 821
Oak Forest, Illinois 60452

Copyright © 2014 Wesley & Neesha Stringfellow
ISBN #978-0-9909348-0-6

Designed & Published by
Heavenly Enterprises Midwest / PublishAffordably.com
service@heavenlyenterprises.com
(773) 783-2981

Dedication

We would like to dedicate this book to our four children. We thank God for each of you and pray a special blessing upon each of you.

To our son Gevon and our beautiful daughter-in-love, Kelani, we thank God for you and for the stand you are taking as a young couple to do everything in your power, with the help of God, to have a healthy marriage and family. We are proud of you and love you dearly. We honor you and our grandbabies, Makenna and Gianna.

To our beautiful daughters Kristen, Danielle, and Nia, we honor the three of you and appreciate the blessing that you are in our lives. God chose us to parent such beautiful and gifted ladies. We pray the blessing of the Lord over your lives, and pray God sends you God-fearing men who will love you and honor you the way that you deserved to be loved. We love you and are proud of you.

Jerry & Chris McQuay

We've been privileged to serve Wes and Neesha Stringfellow as pastors since 2001, and we've seen firsthand their God-given passion for healthy marriages.

They've given freely of their time to help other couples for years, and now through this book, they're able to extend that help beyond a marriage retreat or counseling session.

Even if you don't feel your marriage is in trouble, we should tell you what the experts have told us about our cell phones— that they will work even better if every day or two we just reboot it and give it a chance to restart—to clear out stuff that may have accumulated and caused it to slow it's processes, even if we hadn't noticed. Sometimes even good marriages just need a reboot to be even better.

As pastors, we honestly don't know anyone better to help with that than Wes and Neesha. Chris and I have observed that if you cut them open, they bleed healthy marriages.

We love the fact that Wes and Neesha have been honest here about their struggles and failures, so you can identify yours. Best of all, what they write about is practical—not some psycho-babble you can't even understand—but real-life examples and questions you can use to determine where your marriage is and how it can become the marriage you want.

Thanks, Wes and Neesha, for this gift to married couples in the body of Christ everywhere!

Jerry & Chris McQuay
Christian Life Center

Table of Contents

Dedication .... *i*

From Our Pastors... *iii*

Foreword .... *vii*

Preface .... *xi*

Introduction ....*xiii*

How to Use this Book.. *xxi*

CHAPTER ONE
Strength Assessment 1

CHAPTER TWO
Self-Repair 14

CHAPTER THREE
Spiritual Examination 25

CHAPTER FOUR
Communication..38

CHAPTER FIVE
Intimacy..54

CHAPTER SIX
Financial Unity 68

CHAPTER SEVEN
Investing in Your Marriage...............................81

CHAPTER EIGHT
S.O.S. 89

AFTERWORD
7 Ways To Dump The Junk 96

ONE LAST THING
Firewall Protection 103

Foreword

I can remember coming home one Sunday evening after church service to find about fifty people in my living room. Wes and Neesha had brought many of their church members to my house to have fellowship and prayer. These gatherings began to happen more and more frequently. Sometimes it was a celebration; often, it was no particular occasion; it was a "just because..." Soon, it became apparent to me that something special was being stirred in them: they were bringing people together in the hopes of establishing community among their peers who were believers as they were.

For Wes and Neesha, the most important part of that community began with their married friends. Their greatest desire was that their friends stay together, hang out together, and have their children grow up together. When rifts began to take place within their tight knit group, Wes and Neesha were devastated. They began to have these couples over for dinner, talking, pleading, trying to help them see how important it was for them to stay together. For some, the extra time and attention produced positive results—for others, the breaking had gone too far—they divorced.

This desire to help their friends became a driving force in their lives. They began to study Christian books on marriage. They went to seminars. They prayed. They talked to their friends. Then, they prayed and talked again. With full-time jobs and a young family of their own, they could not give the attention to every couple that needed it. In the midst of their seeking God, I was also petitioning God as to how I could develop opportunities for young and emerging leaders to have a chance to exercise their gifts under guidance. Like upper and lower atmospheric pressure converging together—their passion and my prayers merged to produce Heart to Heart Christian Ministries, now HeartLife Ministries.

Fourteen years ago, our desire to reach people with the message that Jesus Christ could heal and restore your family, no matter how bruised, no matter how broken, has produced an annual Marriage Retreat where hundreds of couples have come to renew, refresh, and sometimes even restore their love for one another. These retreats have not only afforded the couples the opportunity to experience a community of their peers going through similar challenges, but also they receive outstanding teaching on how to guard against the forces that work against them having a happy and satisfying marriage relationship.

Soon it was apparent that once a year was not enough to see change in some marriages. Wes and Neesha again responded to this need by developing an intense "Six Week Boot Camp," designed specifically with strategies and tools to build up the marriage relationship. This book is the written version of just some of the life lessons that they have learned to utilize in their own marriage and what they share with other couples during the boot camp.

As a mother, I am proud of both of them for so faithfully

fulfilling the calling upon their lives. As a visionary, who saw a need for this ministry, I am eternally grateful for their obedience to the Holy Spirit. As a teacher, I marvel at their insight and wisdom and the maturity that it has taken to be transparent before so many. As one who desires to live the servant life, I am challenged by their commitment to serve the "whosoever" God sends their way.

~ Dr. Maria Crawford
Founder of Heartlife Ministries

Marriage Was God's Idea

When you got married, what were your expectations? Whether you married at city hall or had an elaborate wedding, most of us had one main expectation: that we would live "happily ever after." Unless you were privileged to have good counseling prior to your marriage, you walked into marriage, undoubtedly, with blinders on as to what you might face on a daily basis when two independent minds come together as one.

Whatever your experience was, there is one truth that we must remember: MARRIAGE WAS GOD'S IDEA, AND IT STILL IS! Everything God made is good, and on this journey called life, a healthy marriage produces healthy families. If we are going to have a healthy marriage, we must have the proper tools: tools that will keep our marriage running properly. The personal computer has been designed to have a standard operating system that can hold massive amounts of information for long periods of time.

In order to keep that system working effectively, it needs to be rebooted frequently. Marriage can be likened to that computer system – it also needs to be rebooted and rebooted frequently! It is essential that couples take the time to be refreshed, restored, recharged and rebooted!

We have come to offer hope: hope that your marriage will be all that you envision it to be. "Reboot Your Marriage" is more than a systems manual; it is information combined with strategies, inspirational stories and a work-out plan that can give your marriage the extra charge it needs to last a lifetime.

"It Takes Two, Baby"

I recall that at the very beginning of my marriage I made two declarations: the first, that I was going to be happy; and the second, that my marriage was going to be successful. Wes was twenty and I was eighteen when we married. We married sooner than we had originally planned because our first child was on her way.

From the very beginning, I recognized that God's Hand was on our marriage, yet I knew early on that it was going to take me partnering with God in order to achieve my goals. Wes and I both came from very strong family backgrounds even though both of our parents were divorced. We made a mutual decision to do our best to be happy and stay together, and on September 16, 2013 we celebrated twenty-five years of a happy marriage!

Many people spoke words over our marriage, saying that we would not make it through the first five years. After we reached that five years and were still happy, we then heard about the "seven-year itch," and we wondered if there would be any changes to our gifted union. We were still happy. By the time we got to twenty years, we were warned that by that time, most couples, if they were still together, learned to tolerate each other for the sake of the children, drifting into a state of complacency. We did not allow fear to grip us, and while there were challenges, we chose to face them together rather than to disconnect from each other.

The famous Johnnie Taylor sang a song, "It's Cheaper to Keep Her." During those times when we would have a quarrel, I would often say to Wes, "Well, just divorce me, then." His comment would always be, "It's cheaper to keep you!" Now, sometimes this statement would cause us to continue arguing, but over time we learned to end in laughter, realizing that our love was stronger than any obstacle we faced.

Our challenges ran the gamut: from poor financial planning, to learning how to fight for our blended family, to starting and then closing what would appear to be failed business ventures and so much more. But no matter what we faced, we made a choice to remain a team.

Encouragement from others played a major part in the sustained strength of our love. We attended the marriage retreat of some good friends of ours and heard a message spoken by Pastor Darrin Meaders that changed our perspective and has kept us centered; he taught, "It Takes Two, Baby!" In his message, two had a dual meaning, for it spoke not only to the commitment of the two: husband to wife – but also to the intimacy each person in a marriage relationship must have, individually, with our Heavenly Father. While our daily peace and joy is maintained by how well we keep our heavenly connection, the joining of man with woman in marriage was God's idea; therefore, we must keep our relationship with the Creator strong so that every intricate detail of our lives will be strong, including our marriages! It really does, "take two."

The greatest deception that our generation has bought into is that we can make it on our own. No matter how well we appear to be taking care of ourselves, our very next breath, our very next move, are dependent upon the grace of our Daddy. If we trust Him, He will never fail us or let us down. As mere men and women, we may not understand the paths we will have to travel in our marriage, but if we truly recognize that it takes two -- us and our mate AND us and our Heavenly Father walking down the path together—we will know that we are not in it alone. The love of the Father guides us into true intimacy in both our covenant relationship with Him and in our covenant relationship with our spouse. We can have joy throughout our journey, no matter what it brings.

Ecclesiastes says it this way:
It's better to have a partner than go it alone. Share the work, share the wealth. And if one falls down, the other helps, But if there's no one to help, tough! Two in a bed warm each other. Alone, you shiver all night. By yourself you're unprotected. With a friend you can face the worst. Can you round up a third? A three-stranded rope isn't easily snapped. Ecclesiastes 4:9-12 MSG

Neither of you have to be alone – there is someone walking with both of you. By grasping this truth, you will see the difference in every area of your life!

"Let us hold firmly to the hope that we have confessed, because we can trust God to do what He promised..."
Hebrews 10:23

Blessings,
Neesha

The foundation of a marriage is so important. We have witnessed too many marriages where love became dull early in the marriage because the beginning was not built on a solid foundation. Even the very best of us have unforeseen circumstances that can render adverse effects, weakening even a strong marriage. A diminished, or no, income; ineffective communication; intimacy that has grown stale; self-centered spouses; sickness and/or personal tragedies are just a few of the common problems contemporary couples face. Sometimes, seemingly innocent flirtations can become deadly intruders, causing infidelity. These can all lead to what the courts call "irreconcilable differences." Then there are those instances where there are no major problems at all, couples decide that they no longer are in love, and a "no cause" divorce results.

Neesha and I got married at the ages of eighteen and twenty years old. We decided over these past twenty-five years that we were going to make it, no matter what obstacles came our way; and more than that, we were going to enjoy the journey of marriage and not just endure it. All odds were against us: we were expecting our oldest daughter, neither of us had finished college, and we had no jobs. Statistics forecasted that we would never make it to see twenty-five years of marriage.

Our dependence was not on each other but on God first, and then on a strong family who stood with us. They encouraged us, not just with words, but with tangible support as well. We give honor and praise to our Lord and Savior Jesus Christ for giving us the strength to love each other with His love, and then we truly thank God for family and friends who have stood by our sides, especially through those early years.

Our passion for seeing marriages healed was birthed out of the pain of so many of our friends getting divorced. Many people might feel like, "What does this have to do with you?" but it had a lot to do with us, for we saw ourselves as a community. We fellowshipped together at church, went out for social activities together, had babies together, and in general, hung out together all the time.

All of us began our marriages fighting for our families. Yet as young couples, we did not realize the pain that we brought into our marriages: the pain of yesterday's bad experiences, baggage from past relationships, blended families, financial issues, not being able to provide for our mate the kind of intimacy that spoke to him or her. Sadly, many of us never took the time to invest in one of the most precious gifts God has given us: the coming together of a husband and a wife into one, new union.

Many people don't value marriage the way the Bible does. Scripture tells us:

> *Then the LORD God said, "It is not good for the man to be alone. I will make a helper as his complement."*
> *Genesis 2:18 ISV*

Marriages were created by God. We were not put together just to survive but to compliment and love one another, be fruitful and multiply and replenish the earth. We began to understand that this was not just about natural reproduction, but also about reproducing a healthy marriage for the next generation. Far too many believers have allowed the world to define marriage and then wonder about the break-down in our society.

We believe that most couples do want to have a healthy and happy marriage. As with our physical body, we must make healthy choices in order to live. The same is true with the spiritual. The body of Christ needs to put more nutrition, i.e., reinforcement into creating healthy families by focusing on those things that make for a healthy marriage.

The vows we take at the altar are a covenant agreement, made with God first and then with each other. These vows are not just mere words but a solemn promise to give it all and then some: to love each other until death do you part. "Reboot Your Marriage" is a tool that can help bring healing, restoration, and a refreshing into your marriage. Taking the time to go through the re- boot program can help you achieve an enjoyable marriage.

WHY REBOOT?
Whenever we hear the phrase "reboot," we are inclined to think about our material possessions such as batteries, computers, and other kinds of technology. The reboot to which we are referring is a "reboot" or "repair" in your personal life. No, I'm not talking about getting rid of your current spouse and upgrading to a new one; but that is a decision many couple are making, even as you read this page. I am talking about the two of you deciding, together, to put a fresh surge into your marriage. Too many couples feel that it is impossible for them to find happiness in their marriage. If this is you, you have been lied to by the enemy. God wants better for you. He has better plans for your marriage:

For I know the plans I have for you," says the LORD. "They are plans for good and not for disaster, to give you a future and a hope." Jeremiah 29:11 NLT

God spoke to Adam and Even in the Garden of Eden and told them not to eat from the tree of good and evil, but they chose to believe the lie of the serpent and thought there was a better way. They were deceived, just as people in the world are deceived into believing they cannot have a happy marriage.

When Adam and Eve ate from the forbidden tree, God asked them a question:

> *"And He said, 'Who told you that were naked? Have you eaten from the tree that I commanded you not to eat from?'" Genesis 3:11 NIV*

Neesha and I like to ask couples:
Who told you that you can't be married and happy, too?

We have been fed this lie all of our lives from various sources: that it is impossible to be married and happy. Neesha and I have been interacting with couples for over fifteen years, and we've heard this lie and every other one. The thing we find hardest to understand is how people will take the relationship advice of other people, including famous radio and television hosts, without even considering the fact that the person from whom they are soliciting the advice is not in a healthy relationship him or herself. I once asked a single co-worker who was receiving advice on women from another co-worker, one who had been divorced twice and was single at the time, "Whose advice do you really believe: his or mine?" That does not mean by any stretch of the imagination that people who have been divorced can't give sound advice on relationships, but when you want to understand how something works, isn't it better to go to someone who has figured out how to make it work?

We can make healthy choices which will pay huge dividends. Invest in your marriage by going on retreats and getaways. Get involved in married groups at your church. Neesha and I try to absorb as much knowledge on marriage as possible so that our relationship can stay healthy and enjoyable. That was God's original plan for us. He wanted man to have a companion; He did not just want us to have a roommate for the sake of convenience or "for the good of the children."

Speaking of children, they are watching us; they see and feel everything that is going on in our homes, and it does affect them in one way or another. Every parent who is reading this would likely say that they would lay down their lives for their kids. Well, how about deciding to "live for them," instead? I would like to believe that my son, who got married at the age of twenty-three, is looking at my marriage as an example of what a happy marriage looks like. I believe my son knows his marriage will be great because he had a good role model to look up to.

You too, can find a way to make your marriage a happy one, not only for yourselves, but also for the health and well-being of your children, and your children's children. No matter what road you are on, know that God can see you through. He can give you joy in the midst of your journey, no matter what is on your road.

In this book, we will help you discover the tools that will provide strength in your marriage: Self-Repair, Spiritual Examination, Effective Communication, True Intimacy, Financial Unity, and Investing in your Marriage.

We are excited that you have joined us and look forward to traveling together on a journey that will lead us to a healthy, successful marriage.

Blessings,
Wes

How To Use This Book

Reboot your Marriage was designed to rejuvenate marriages and to give you a fire that will rekindle your desire to have a long-lasting, fun-filled journey together. There are several different approaches for this text that we recommend. You might use this book for:

- Individual Couples Study
- Marriage Seminars
- Six-Week Marriage Reboot Camp Programs*

While the work of the reboot is challenging, the process of the reboot is simple. Regardless of the delivery format, you will:

1. Take the strength assessment survey, finding out where you are individually as well as learning if you are on the same page as your spouse. Knowing who and where you each are is critical for this process.

2. Do a self-repair check. People often blame their spouse and forget all about what they need to do as an individual. This check will alleviate some of the pressure to find scapegoats for our personal issues.

3. Understanding that we can't fix ourselves, we will then take our evaluation to our Heavenly Father as we go through a spiritual examination.

4. The spiritual examination will allow us grace to repent from the areas where we falter and then ask God to heal the brokenness, showing us where we need to make changes.

5. Once we can see clearly because the Heavenly Father has shown us ourselves, and we are on our way to healing, we can communicate with each other as our true selves.

6. In this communication, we can begin to talk about what our needs, desires and dreams are. The communication is not a one-sided street, so we can't be only a talker and not a listener. We also have to find out what language we speak: what makes us frown; what makes us smile.

7. Growing and improving our communication will lead to intimacy, a connection that clearly says, "You see my heart, know my desires and are determined to be close to me in a way that will bring passion and love." Growth is inevitable at this point.

8. With the free flow of love birthed from the previous steps, you will be in a good place to begin speaking about your financial unity. If you still can't seem to agree or find there is not unity in your finances, which in turn affects your communication, by all means seek out a mediator—someone who can allow you both to listen and to help you reach your common goal.

9. After you have discerned appropriate financial investments, you will determine how to further invest in your marriage as a unit.

We are excited that you have joined us and look forward to partnering with you as we strengthen our relationships; examine our past hurts and get healing for our wounds; communicate our feelings more effectively; become free financially; rekindle our intimacy; and invest in God's idea… marriage.

* Wes and Neesha Stringfellow of Heartlife Ministries are available to train individuals as well as large groups in the Marriage ReBoot Camp format. Please contact the authors for more details for this service.

Starting With Prayer

~ Dear Heavenly Father,
We thank and praise You for our marriage covenant. We are asking that You will refresh our marriage. Open our hearts that we may receive all You have for us. Our hearts' desire is for our marriage to be pleasing in Your sight, that You might get the glory from our union.

Help us to be an example to other couples and to share the good news that marriages can be filled with love, passion and joy. We can have a blessed marriage.

Most importantly, let all that we learn allow us to have the best marriage ever.

In Jesus' Name,
Amen

CHAPTER ONE

Strength Assessment

"I don't know about you, but I'm running hard for the finish line. I'm giving it everything I've got. No sloppy living for me! I'm staying alert and in top condition. I'm not going to get caught napping, telling everyone else all about it and then missing out myself." 1 Corinthians 9:27 MSG

THE STORY ~

Being the eldest of eight children was bad enough, but then, I never really felt very smart. Although I grew up in a Christian, God-fearing home, there was still emptiness. I accepted Christ at an early age, and I knew he had a plan for my life; it was just not going the way I had dreamed that it would go. I experienced all types of rejection in both grammar school and in high school and struggled with low self-esteem. I never felt pretty or that I would measure up to the people whom I desired to be my peers.

Young men in the church that I was very fond of only had one thing in mind, and because I was not experienced in the area of promiscuity, I was rejected, again. As crazy as it sounds, I got stood up my senior year in high school for our prom. Very soon after, I learned that my parents' marriage was not on good terms. I did not understand all of the dynamics, but I trusted God to heal their relationship. Unfortunately, it takes two to realize and admit the weak areas in your life, and their relationship did not make it. I became pregnant a year after meeting Wes, and although we got married right away, as a young, pregnant, unmarried leader in church, I suffered lots of ridicule from family and friends. It was a very painful experience, and needless to say, I experienced more rejection.

I suppressed it to move on with my life because the joy I had with my husband outweighed all of tears of yesterday; however, I will admit: you don't truly realize what areas you are weak in until you do an assessment of your life, which definitely lead to Wes and I doing a strength assessment of our marriage. In what areas were we weak? Strong? What things did I struggle with which had developed pre-marriage?

There were things that I did not share with him because I had no idea they existed. Shame, fear and rejection all played a part in my behavior! And all of these kinds of things show up sooner or later in a marriage. They showed up in ours, but talking about them and being open and transparent was inevitable if we were going to have a healthy marriage. Every marriage should do a strength assessment. You can only heal if you reveal the truth: the truth of your experiences in life, pre marriage.

Confess your faults one to another, and pray one for another, that ye may be healed. The effectual fervent prayer of a righteous man availeth much. James 5:16

~

STRENGTH ASSESSMENT

Discovering where you "are" is one of the first steps to having a healthy relationship. Human nature tends to cause us to ignore our own personal weaknesses and instead point the finger at our spouse, yet understanding the true meaning of a healthy relationship begins with being honest with ourselves. When two people come together, there are two different minds, two different personalities, two different backgrounds. Recognizing that you and your spouse may think differently does not at all mean that you cannot have the same goals or be on the same page; in fact, this is the first step to achieving a healthy marriage. This book is designed for couples who want to commit to doing what it takes to have a healthy marriage. Making a commitment and being willing to understand where you are as an individual and as a couple is essential.

When we go to the gym to work out, we often begin with an assessment to find out our strengths and weaknesses. The physical journey to getting your body into shape and becoming healthy can be challenging; however, the more you practice and exercise, the stronger you become. You begin to build muscle and you can take on more resistance. Building a healthy marriage requires the same practice: developing strength in our weak places. Some couples want to give up at the onset, feeling that the marriage workouts are too strenuous. Yet, we have found that, as in the physical, if there is continuous repetition of the same exercises, over time you will see muscles develop in your marriage, and you will be encouraged to embark upon a road that will make your marriage healthy and happy, too!

A successful marriage must have honest communication, diligence, and endurance. It is our desire that by the time you have finished this book, you will see and understand each other with new eyes, fall more deeply in love, and become a living example of what God intended for marriages to be. The decision has to be made by both of you, that you are a team, in it for the long haul until death do you part.

Now, because none of us begin with the same level of endurance, we have to identify our own unique weaknesses and then concentrate on exercises that will build endurance for those areas, creating a strong foundation for any issues we may come against. The parable in Matthew 7:25 MSG illustrates that no matter how bad the storm is, your house will not be moved it if is set upon a solid rock:

> *These words I speak to you are not incidental additions to your life, homeowner improvements to your standard of living. They are foundational words, words to build a life on. If you work these words into your life, you are like a smart carpenter who built his house on solid rock. Rain poured down, the river flooded, a tornado hit—but nothing moved that house. It was fixed to the rock.*

Life, no matter how well we plan, has a way of throwing us unexpected curves. From financial problems to family problems, life happens and can give us a crash course on just how differently we view life as individuals. No matter how many difficulties come our way, we must really believe that God can see us through and can give us the assurance that we are overcomers. God wants to give us joy in the midst of our journey. By remaining committed to God, to each other and to the reboot process, you too will have joy. Assessing your strengths is the first step in that process.

Rating Your Marriage
Every couple should take the time to rate their marriage. Go ahead and try it; give your marriage a grade. But before you

do, ask yourself:

- What is it like being married to me?

Every couple needs to participate in this exercise because while you may think all is well, that may not necessarily be the case. It is just like weighing yourself or taking your blood pressure; checking these vital statistics periodically helps to you stay healthy. Marriage is the same way. Are things piling up that are weighing you down? Are you functioning on a day-to-day basis in a way that is healthy? Or, are you just operating in survival mode, headed for a break-down? Take the time to first ask yourself:

- How am I doing as a spouse?
- Am I fulfilling my role in our relationship?

Please understand: love, passion, and romance tend to diminish if you do not make regular assessments. Being in love with your spouse is very important, however, liking your spouse is equally important. Couples can say, "I love you" every day but may discover over time that they don't like each other. Consider these questions:

- Are you friends with each other?
- Do you communicate effectively?
- How often do you quarrel?

Honest responses will help you determine where you are in your marriage, yet don't forget that your questioning must begin with yourself. Before you point the finger and address every character flaw your spouse has, take the time to give yourself a check-up.

- How are things going with me?

Another important question is:

- Do you see yourself growing old together?

This is a question that should automatically be a YES, and if it is not, you really need a REBOOT!

- How do others view my marriage?

Now, we have definitely faced some opposition with this question, and we have heard it said over and over, "I don't care what others think of my marriage, as long as I think we are good."

Our response to this is: yes and no!

Yes, you should care because you are:

> *"... (our) epistle written in our hearts, known and read of all men." 2 Corinthians 3:2*

You should be striving to give the world an example of a healthy marriage. Healthy marriages create healthy children, families, churches, societies, and ultimately, they have the potential for creating a healthy world. So, yes, you should care what others think about your marriage to the extent that you are putting your best foot forward, setting a standard to be the best you can be in your marriage.

But there is also a "no." You should not care what others think if they say you are corny or lame for creating a safe and healthy environment for your family. No, you should not care if people think you are strange or unrealistic by establishing boundaries and not following the world's pattern of what it thinks marriage should be. Setting a standard is not popular, but it can become contagious if your goal is taking a stand to have the best marriage ever.

Rating the Marriages You Know

Rating your parent's marriage can help you determine why you treat your spouse and/or react to your marriage the way you do. Your upbringing has a lot to do with your successes or failures in many areas of your life. Ideally, people use the disappointments of their past to make them better, stronger individuals. Unfortunately, there are people who never heal from their yesterdays, they bring the bondage of generational habits into all of their relationships, especially marriage.

The responses you give or don't give; the way you handle conflict; the way you express or don't express passion; withholding information, keeping secrets, and many other intentional or unintentional habits are oftentimes learned from your parents. In their relationship, they either developed ways which helped make their marriage stronger, or they practiced behaviors that made it weaker, or even dissolved it.

Children observe many things that are reflected involuntarily in their future behaviors. Young love believes that it can overcome anything, and the excitement of that young love may cause us to even forget the witnessed actions and behaviors. One of the things we have learned is that, eventually, what is in you will come out. Rebooting your marriage helps couples discover and then address the weak areas, keeping at bay the unresolved issues of your collective past.

Every strength assessment points out the weak areas and places that need to be built up. This is the time to be honest, even if you are struggling. Putting up a front that you are healthy, when you are not, will eventually become obvious. So make sure you are honest and transparent: honest with yourself and transparent with God and your spouse. As you begin to put healthy habits into practice, you will develop a stronger relationship with God and definitely with your spouse.

ACTIVITY

STRENGTH ASSESSMENT SURVEY

Separately, complete the survey which follows, from your heart. Make sure that you each take the time to think about how you really see your marriage. Remember, honesty is one of the greatest keys to a healthy marriage. Circle your best response or respond in the space provided.

Husband's Strength Assessment Survey

1. How would you rate your marriage?
   A. Healthy and in excellent condition
   B. A little out of shape, needs some work
   C. Completely out of shape
   D. What marriage?

2. I like my spouse
   A. All the time
   B. Most of the time
   C. Some of the time
   D. Not much at all

3. Do you see yourself growing old together?
   A. All the time
   B. Most of the time
   C. Some of the time
   D. Not at all

4. How would you rate your parent's marriage on a scale of 1-10? (one, the lowest, 10 being the highest) Why?

_____

_____

5. On a scale of 1-10, what is it like being married to me?

_____

_____

6. The keys to a healthy marriage are:

A._____

B._____

C._____

7. My spouse's main needs and desires are: (wants or likes)

A._____

B._____

C._____

8. My main needs and desires are:

A._____

B._____

C._____

9. I have problems in these areas:

A._____

B._____

C._____

10. I demonstrate my love by:

   A._____

   B._____

   C._____

11. These are the areas I know I can improve in my marriage:

   A._____

   B._____

   C._____

12. List three goals you hope to achieve while you reboot your marriage:

   A._____

   B._____

   C._____

Next Steps:
When you have completed your survey, compare your answers with your spouse's answers. While keeping an open mind, be willing to discuss them openly and honestly.

Wife's Strength Assessment Survey

1. How would you rate your marriage?

   A. Healthy and in excellent condition

   B. A little out of shape, needs some work

   C. Completely out of shape

   D. What marriage?

2. I like my spouse
   A. All the time

   B. Most of the time

   C. Some of the time

   D. Not much at all

3. Do you see yourself growing old together?
   A. All the time

   B. Most of the time

   C. Some of the time

   D. Not at all

4. How would you rate your parent's marriage on a scale of 1-10? (one, the lowest, 10 being the highest) Why?

   _____

   _____

5. On a scale of 1-10, what is it like being married to me?

   _____

   _____

6. The keys to a healthy marriage are:
   A._____

   B._____

   C._____

7. My spouse's main needs and desires are: (wants or likes)
   A._____

   B._____

   C._____

8. My main needs and desires are:

   A. _____

   B. _____

   C. _____

9. I have problems in these areas:

   A. _____

   B. _____

   C. _____

10. I demonstrate my love by:

    A. _____

    B. _____

    C. _____

11. These are the areas I know I can improve in my marriage:

    A. _____

    B. _____

    C. _____

12. List three goals you hope to achieve while you reboot your marriage:

    A. _____

    B. _____

    C. _____

Next Steps:
When you have completed your survey, compare your answers with your spouse's answers. While keeping an open mind, be willing to discuss them openly and honestly.

Finally, brethren, whatsoever things are true, whatsoever things are noble, whatsoever things are just, whatsoever things are pure, whatsoever things are lovely, whatsoever things are of good report, if there be any virtue, and if there be anything praiseworthy, meditate on these things. Philippians 4:8

~ CHAPTER TWO ~

Self-Repair

"Wherefore seeing we also are compassed about with so great a cloud of witnesses, let us lay aside every weight, and the sin which doth so easily beset us, and let us run with patience the race that is set before us." Hebrews 12:1

And that's about it, friends. Be cheerful. Keep things in good repair. Keep your spirits up. Think in harmony. Be agreeable. Do all that, and the God of love and peace will be with you for sure. Greet one another with a holy embrace. All the brothers and sisters here say hello. 2 Corinthians 13:11-13

THE STORY ~

We worked in ministry nonstop, and we worked our jobs; we were blessed. God continued to smile on our marriage: we purchased our home, began to invest, and everything seemed great, but then little things started to happen with Neesha where she would attack me and snap at me for no apparent reason. I thought to myself, among other things, "What is wrong with this woman?" I began to let her know my thoughts: "Woman, you need some help." Neesha was offended, as any spouse would be, if they constantly heard that they needed to get some psychiatric help or counseling. I told her, "But you are blaming me for things that don't even have anything to do with me!" The conversations we were having were not making sense.

I am thankful to God that Neesha has always been the type of person to work on herself because she began to seek help. She left the offenses and realized that there was some hidden pain she had not dealt with, be it from her childhood or teenage years. It could not have been much more, simply because we had gotten married so young. Thank God for counselors; we always say, "The best counselors need counseling."

~

There was point in my life where I had to forgive myself and my past. It began with me reaching a point where I would snap at my husband spontaneously, often without cause. I began to get offended with every little thing he said and the way he said it. I especially began to get offended when he would tell me that I needed to get some professional help.

Frustrated by his continuous comments, I decided to seek out wise counsel. What I discovered was that I had so much unforgiveness in my heart. I was hurt by many things I had experienced during my childhood and teenage years. I was still walking in condemnation about getting pregnant and not keeping my virginity. I was clearly embarrassed about having what the world calls a "shotgun" wedding. I was frustrated with not finishing college and being tormented by the insecurities of never measuring up to what people expected of me. All of these things lead to suppressed pain—pain that would not show up until later in life. And who caught the brunt of the pain? Correct. Wes did. I didn't realize that there was so much I was carrying. As I continued my sessions, I learned that I was walking in unforgiveness in many areas of my life.

I made a choice to forgive: first to forgive myself and then the others who had no idea that they had even done anything wrong. It was not until I made this choice and decided to become healthy, that I noticed a change in my home, my husband, my children and others around me.

Even today, I have come to realize that I need to revisit self-repair over and over. There are so many issues we have that we don't realize might resurface: the issues we thought we had overcome and the ones we didn't even recognize still existed. I thank God for constantly allowing me to know that there is so much more to be dealt with. And so my journey continues…

~

BEGINNING THE JOURNEY
This is one of my favorite scriptures:

> *Create in me a clean heart, O God; and renew a right spirit within me. Psalms 51:10*

It is such a simple verse, yet it appears to be one of the hardest processes in the world for people to go through, especially in marriage: learning to let go and learning to be free. When you hold onto things and choose not to forgive, it affects every area of your life, and you will not be able to fulfill the true plan God has for you. You will not have a happy marriage and your unforgiveness will spread like a cancer to your children.

Today choose to forgive. Choose to be free! Confess aloud:
"I must."
"I will."

"I have forgiveness."

We must pray and ask God to forgive us and help us to move on. Know that this is the only way to have a "whole," happier you, a healthy life, and a healthy marriage. He is a God who will definitely do what you ask.

YOUR SELF-REPAIR
"And you will know the truth, and the truth will set you free." John 8:32 NLT

Whenever your computer is not operating to its full potential, the first thing you do is run a diagnostic on the system, looking for errors or viruses that may have attached themselves. Most of these viruses come from outside sources due to the lack of a proper protection plan, like a good anti-virus program. "Bad stuff" in equals "bad stuff" out.

The purpose of this chapter is to discover our own personal flaws, recognize the areas in which we are weak, acknowledge them, and then ask God for healing. The majority of people we have encountered in our ministry tend to blame their spouses for the problems in their marriage while failing to focus on the flaws generated by the areas needing repair in their own lives.

DO I NEED IMPROVEMENT?
Asking yourself this question means you understand that there are issues which have affected you and your life relationships. If our spouse asks us where we think they need improvement, we can usually shoot out a list without even giving it much thought. Examining ourselves, however, can be more difficult, because in most cases, acknowledgment of these issues signals inside of us that change is needed. Fortunately, simply recognizing that improvement is needed is half of the battle.

ACTIVITY

THE **S**TRUGGLE IS **R**EAL

Answer the following questions about your personal struggles. Be open and honest to begin your road to self-repair.

Struggles don't always have to be disastrous, but are clearly things you can change because they hinder your relationship from being healthy.

In what areas do I know that I struggle and have a desire to change? _____

_____

_____

_____

Would my spouse agree with me?_____

_____

_____

_____

_____

After making our list of areas for change, it is good to focus on the greatest need first, i.e., that area that appears, most frequently, to be troublesome. Often, by improving just this one area, the other problems on your list can be diminished or even eliminated.

Will Your Spouse Agree With Your List? _____

Being honest with oneself—honest enough to desire and to seek change—is critical. Sometimes our spouses will agree with our list of areas we need to change, and sometimes they will see other areas as being the problem. Some of our spouses are not yet honest enough with themselves to begin their own change process. They also might think that the areas you perceive as major are not really that major at all. It is important to address your personal areas of concern if they are important to you, and even if they do not seem important to your mate. As you begin to rectify the identified problem areas, you will be better able to accept further constructive opinions or criticism from others. Now, please remember: you must afford your mate the same opportunity to make adjustments and changes as you are being afforded. The grace to go through the change process is vital for both partners.

We believe that it is the work of the Holy Spirit that begins to reveal areas in your life that are unsettled. That same Holy Spirit will lead and guide us into all truth. God's love for us brings us to the realization of the truth and then breathes upon us the desire to change and the strength to be healed! Healing is important, yet while only God can heal, we have to recognize the need for God, allow Him to show us the root of our problems, and then rely upon Him to heal us.

TO HEAL AND TO REPAIR:
Establishing a Common Frame of Reference
Let's establish a common frame of reference by looking at some definitions. The Merriam Webster on-line dictionary gives these definition:

Heal:

1a. to make sound or whole; heal a wound

b. to restore to health

2a. to cause (an undesirable condition) to be overcome

b. to patch up (a breach or division); heal a breach between friends

3. a. to restore to original purity or integrity; healed of sin

Repair:

1. To restore to sound condition after damage or injury; fix, repaired the broken watch

2. To set right; remedy: repair an oversight

3. To renew or revitalize

4. To make up for or compensate for

You must truly internalize the meanings of these terms in order to move forward in your process. There is no repair without healing; there is no healing without repair. They work hand-in-hand.

SIGNS THAT POINT TO A NEED FOR REPAIR

Has there ever been a time in your life when you didn't want to deal with situations? Have you ever made any of these statements?

- I don't need any counseling
- I am not ready
- Not now, but I will soon
- I just am not ready to deal with it right now
- I'm good

They are clear signs that a person needs repair.

Sometimes spouses even begin to blame each other for their

pain, when in actuality, there is some self-repair that needs to take place. When self-repair is needed there are some visible signs that a spouse might display. He or she might:

1. Appear to be on top of the game, even if he or she is not

2. Take great pains to maintain a certain public image

3. Put up walls to keep people out

PUTTING ON BAND-AIDS
Many couples put a Band-Aid on their problems, fixing things temporarily just in order to move on, never really addressing the real issues. Often the issues are very small and can be rectified by taking the time to communicate how each person feels. If you let the problem sit and fester however, it will turn into a mountain of infection. Sometimes that infection cannot be treated without extraordinary intervention.

There are some easy rules to incorporate into your lives that can help:

1. Take the time you need to talk to your spouse about the smallest of problems.

2. Never get too busy to share your heart.

3. Share with each other, and not with outside voices who mean you no good.

4. Don't allow shame to keep you in hiding. Shame will produce years of insanity until you look up one day and decide you can't handle it anymore.

FORGIVENESS: THE TRUE ROAD TO SELF-REPAIR
One of the greatest hurdles we may ever have to leap over is unforgiveness. Unforgiveness in our heart is like a parasite in our blood draining all the vital nutrients we need to be healthy. We must learn to forgive ourselves and then learn to forgive the other people in our past and present who have

wronged us, including our spouses.

The question is:

• How do I get to that place?

• How can I feel happy again?

It is possible; you can get there. Yes, even now, you are on the way!

No one likes to be held hostage for something they have done. No one wants a constant reminder that they are wrong. Everyone would love for their slate to be wiped clean. You can always tell whether or not you have forgiven the person in question when the situation you have forgiven is no longer a problem for you. You can talk about it, share it with others, and actually allow the experience to be a testimony for others.

We have watched countless talk shows over the years with people who have come forth, forgiving rapists, molesters, parents who had failed them, husbands and wives who cheated, and so much more. Each one of these people had to make a choice not only to forgive, but to become public with their forgiveness. They had to decide to let it go so they could become a healthier person.

Harboring things in your past is not only painful for you, but for those around you. Unchecked, the parasite of unforgiveness becomes a cancer with one main goal: death. That parasite will not only kill you but kill the relationships around you. How? Because when the host, you or your spouse, holds onto the pain, it eventually turns into bitterness, resentment, depression, hostility and other destructive feelings that sabotage those relationships.

It is very important in our lives, whether married or single, divorced or a widow, to let things go and not to hold onto yesterday. God knew that this concept would be difficult for mankind, seeing the way things would go before they happened, so He gave us the ultimate benefit of forgiving others:

> *For if you forgive men their trespasses, our heavenly Father will also forgive you. Matthew 6:14*

PRAYERS THAT REPAIR
Spend some time with the Father talking to Him about your self-repair needs.

Honesty and surrender to God
~ Dear Heavenly Father,
    I acknowledge that I have harbored things in my heart that have kept me from being close to You and from surrendering my heart to You. Please forgive me today of my sins; forgive me from my past hurts and pains. I receive the healing that You bore on Calvary's cross. Thank You, Heavenly Father, for my healing.

                              In Jesus' Name, Amen

Honesty with yourself
~ Dear Heavenly Father,
    I surrender my heart, mind, and soul to You. I recognize that I have fear, unforgiveness, and unresolved pain in my heart. I realize that it has caused me to be an unhealthy individual. Please take the pain away and make me brand new. I claim 2 Corinthians 5:17 as mine: "If any man be in Christ, he is a new creature, old things are passed away and all things are becoming new."

                              In Jesus' Name, Amen

Honesty with your spouse
~ Dear Heavenly Father,
I come to You asking You to give me the words and wisdom to communicate with my spouse. I know they might not understand everything I have been through and what areas I need to repair, but please lead and guide me with the words of love to let them know that I am on a path of healing. Thank You for helping them understand how to pray for me as Your Word becomes clear and as I yield completely to Your Voice.

In Jesus' Name, Amen

When you become honest with yourself, then and only then can God move on your behalf. Self-repair is not fixing yourself; it is being honest about the true issues plaguing you on the inside. We must be willing to bring the tears in our heart to God, asking Him to progress this journey of spiritual examination and advance our healing.

~ CHAPTER THREE ~

Spiritual Examination

Examine yourselves, whether ye be in the faith; prove your own selves. Know ye not your own selves, how that Jesus Christ is in you, except ye be reprobates? 2 Corinthians 13:5

Investigate my life, O God, find out everything about me; Cross-examine and test me, get a clear picture of what I'm about; See for yourself whether I've done anything wrong—then guide me on the road to eternal life. Psalm 139:23-24 MSG

We justify our actions by appearances; GOD examines our motives. Proverbs 21:2 MSG

THE STORY ~

"Just divorce me, then," I would say, as arguments and spats arose in our marriage. I did not believe in physical fighting, but words were my thing. I didn't understand that I wasn't supposed to throw out digs or comments that might leave my spouse broken.

One scripture that comes to mind is Matthew 12:34 NKJV:

"...For the mouth speaks what the heart is full of...How can you, being evil, speak good things? For out of the abundance of the heart, the mouth speaks..." What's inside of you, including your thoughts and unspoken words will come out eventually, either verbally or through your actions. One of the ways I would always respond to my hurt was to say, "Well, just divorce me"; I made this comment so often during the beginning of our marriage because I was afraid that Wes only married me because I was pregnant; then, when we would disagree, I always felt like he didn't want to stay.

This was not the case at all, and after about five years of repeatedly making the comment over and over again, I realized that I was tearing down my own marriage. God dealt with me and I stopped saying it.

I never really wanted a divorce, after all; I just wanted to hear Wes say that he didn't want a divorce. Of course, he was stubborn and would only let me know that after we made up. As frustrating as it was, I came to learn that there was a better way to deal with arguments than to make comments that I really didn't mean. Throwing out digs was just digging me into a deeper ditch. I thank God for my consistent relationship with Christ because I found myself constantly repenting and asking God to blot out my transgressions, forgive me, examine me and make my heart pure.

Then there was the "no church" issue because Wes didn't want to go to church. I grew up in the church; that had been my entire life, yet I loved my husband, so I began to stay home with him. I was tired of asking, begging, and even sometimes trying to use manipulative ways to get him there. I will never forget when God spoke to me and told me, "WHILE YOU ARE WAITING ON WES, I AM WAITING ON YOU."

I was spooked because I heard it like someone was talking to me, directly. I had never heard God speak so powerfully to me. It scared me but it got my attention, too, and on Sunday morning, I went to church. God lead me to a church where the pastors were caring and loving, and I began to share with the Pastor's wife how frustrated I was in coming to church alone. It had only been a couple of months, but I told her that I was just going to join without Wes. She told me, "Just wait on God; Wes will come." As a matter of fact, she basically told me that she would not accept my membership until Wes came with me. I told her, "Oh well, we will be waiting."

I had no intention of trusting God, but within two weeks of that conversation, Wes came to church with me and completely surrendered his heart to God. I learned a valuable lesson: God was waiting on MY surrender. I was so busy worrying about Wes while God was waiting on me to answer. I did and He showed up. The one thing I learned is while you are requesting God to examine you, heal you, and work it out for you, there is patience involved. I had to trust Him and not do things my own way.

> *Trust in the Lord with all of your heart and lean not to your own understanding, but in all your ways acknowledge Him, and He will direct your path. Psalm 3:5,6*

Direction comes from our Heavenly Father, and He will allow you to heal and change: a valuable lesson that I have learned and am still learning.

PREPARING FOR SPIRITUAL EXAMINATION

- Are you pretending?
- Is your faith genuine?

- Are you living or just going through the motions?
- Have you embraced the true call and purpose of your marriage?

The Word of God calls for constant examination of the believer:

Put me on trial, Lord, and cross-examine me. Test my motives and my heart. Psalm 26:2 NLT

Even the Apostle Paul devotes time to the process of spiritual examination in relation to the power of Christ's sacrifice for mankind and His expectations for our behavior:

Well, this is my third visit coming up. Remember the Scripture that says, "A matter becomes clear after two or three witnesses give evidence"? On my second visit I warned that bunch that keeps sinning over and over in the same old ways that when I came back I wouldn't go easy on them. Now, preparing for the third, I'm saying it again from a distance. If you haven't changed your ways by the time I get there, look out. You who have been demanding proof that Christ speaks through me will get more than you bargain for. You'll get the full force of Christ, don't think you won't. He was sheer weakness and humiliation when he was killed on the cross, but oh, he's alive now—in the mighty power of God! We weren't much to look at, either, when we were humiliated among you, but when we deal with you this next time, we'll be alive in Christ, strengthened by God.

Test yourselves to make sure you are solid the faith. Don't drift along taking everything for granted. Give yourselves regular checkups. You need firsthand evidence, not mere hearsay that Jesus Christ is in you. Test it out. If you fail the test, do something about it. I hope the test won't show that we have failed. But if it comes to that, we'd rather the test shows our failure than yours. We're rooting for the truth to win out in you. We couldn't possibly do otherwise. We don't just put up with our limitations; we celebrate them, and then go on to celebrate every strength, every triumph of the truth in you. We pray hard that it will all come together in your lives.

I'm writing this to you now so when I come I won't have to say another word on the subject. The authority the Master gave me is putting people together, not taking them apart. I want to get on with it, and not have to spend time on reprimands.

And that's about it, friends. Be cheerful. Keep things in good repair. Keep your spirits up. Think in harmony. Be agreeable. Do all that, and the God of love and peace will be with you for sure. Greet one another with a holy embrace. All the brothers and sisters here say hello.

The amazing grace of the Master, Jesus Christ, the extravagant love of God, the intimate friendship of the Holy Spirit, is with all of you. 2 Corinthians 13 MSG

THE JOURNEY THAT LEADS TO HEALING

Now that you have been honest about your journey and recognize the areas that need to be repaired, rejoice in the freedom of knowing that you are well on your way to rebooting yourself and your marriage. When healing comes to an individual, it changes everything and everyone around you. It took me a long time to realize that everyone in my life is affected by me. My spouse, my family, and my friends had to go on my healing journey with me because of the effect that it had on me. God is the Repairman; when we ask Him to both examine us and heal us, He is able to do just that! He is the Creator and knows us better than we know ourselves. Embrace your journey, stay on the path, and whatever you do, don't get side-tracked from being totally and completely healed.

SPIRITUAL EXAMINATION

When preparing for an examination: with the doctor, school testing, or a diagnostic exam on your car, there is a tendency to be nervous about the outcome. If you are the type of person that likes to be in control, you might really be concerned if there is a problem with the exam. The question we ask first is Will I pass the exam?

Yet, how many times in our marriage do we fail the test before us because we fear that we are not in control? The need to be in control sets our spouse up for failure and sets us up for disappointment. Two individuals will not always think alike or respond to life's situations in the same way. When we set unreasonable expectations, and then blame our spouse when they don't respond or can't deliver, then we are disappointed. But was the thing for which we hoped realistic?

Then there are those situations when we as women want our husbands to be mind readers. We have a certain desire and we expect our spouse to be able to fill in the blanks to prove their love for us. This is one of the prime ways we set our spouses up for failure. Remember: An unfair expectation yields an unfair failure.

These situations, when they become apparent to us after spiritual examination, are definitely areas where we need to ask God to intervene.

On this road of spiritual examination, you might find that there are many times when you will want to give up. It is much easier to avoid what needs to be fixed rather than to dive in and fix it. We've all experienced leaky faucets: first, you just hear the annoying drip; then, you find a puddle which begins to cause damage; finally, you call a plumber who has to go in and dismantle everything, often replacing all of the old pipes and cleaning out all of the toxic waste that has accumulated with the leak.

The Holy Spirit is a Master Plumber. He will show you areas in your life that need to be repaired and healed. When He examines us, we never know what might show up, but we can be sure of one thing: He does not do a half job. God does all things well.

WHEN YOU HAVE TO DO IT ALONE

Couples do not always arrive at the same conclusions at the same time. When you come to the conclusion that you need to embark upon your journey to healing, you must do it, even if you have to do it without the support of your spouse. When you try to force healing on someone else who may not be ready, you might hear phrases like this:

- I don't need counseling.

- I don't have any problems; I'm not interested in dealing with the past, and I'm just looking forward to the future.

- I don't want to go to a marriage retreat.

- I have tried to change. I am what I am and I'm just done.

- I refuse to waste my time trying to see change; it's not worth it.

Pride will keep a person from seeking help that they know they need. However, if you allow another person to stop you from getting the help you need, you will fall victim to that same spirit of pride. Having a spirit of pride will keep you stranded and handicap your growth.

"Pride goes before destruction and a haughty spirit before a fall." Proverbs 16:18

SIGNS OF PRIDE

Pride does not masquerade with high heels on. It is a subtle spirit that feeds upon the hidden resentment we have when we feel like we're not appreciated. Consider these typical responses that we use to justify why we do what we do:

- Well, I am normally the one who gives

- I'm not the one with the problem; my spouse is

- I'll try to forgive you, but I won't ever forget

While these responses are natural, they are neither healthy nor productive for healing or ownership of our personal growth.

STEPS TO RECOVERY

You can start the process to recovery by praying daily for you and your spouse. Paul's advice to Timothy in I Timothy 4:7 was to, "…Discipline yourself for the purpose of godliness." When you recognize the areas that need repair and healing:

1. Write them down (look at them and pray for healing).

2. Acknowledge your desire to be healed.

3. Move forward by taking the necessary steps to becoming healthy.

4. Seek wise counsel.

5. Frequently examine the progress you have made and appreciate it.

6. Rejoice in victories and testimonies.

7. Respect that just as you can change, other people, including your spouse, can change, too.

Willingness

As you progress, things will undoubtedly become more challenging. During the strenuous times of testing, we must continue to press in, even when it is uncomfortable. We must keep before us the repairs that must be done and receive the healing the Holy Spirit wants to bring to us. Most importantly, we have to resist the urge to point the finger at others, reminding ourselves of the Words of Jesus found in Matthew 7:3-11 MSG:

"Don't pick on people, jump on their failures, criticize their faults—unless, of course, you want the same treatment. That critical spirit has a way of boomeranging. It's easy to see a smudge on your neighbor's face and be oblivious to the ugly sneer on your own. Do you have the nerve to say, 'Let me wash your face for you,' when your own face is distorted by contempt? It's this whole traveling road-show mentality all over again, playing a holier-than-thou part instead of just living your part. Wipe that ugly sneer off your own face, and you might be fit to offer a washcloth to your neighbor."

"Don't be flip with the sacred. Banter and silliness give no honor to God. Don't reduce holy mysteries to slogans. In trying to be relevant, you're only being cute and inviting sacrilege.

"Don't bargain with God. Be direct. Ask for what you need. This isn't a cat-and-mouse, hide-and-seek game we're in. If your child asks for bread, do you trick him with sawdust? If he asks for fish, do you scare him with a live snake on his plate? As bad as you are, you wouldn't think of such a thing. You're at least decent to your own children. So don't you think the God who conceived you in love will be even better?

The fight is worth it! We don't always understand that the past is affecting our present actions, yet when the knowledge of an issue has surfaced, it can positively change the entire pattern of our behavior emotionally, physically, spiritually, mentally, and sexually.

Couples should care about the well-being of each other's spiritual life, however the best thing you could ever do for one another is to pray and be patient while waiting on God to move. While you are praying and waiting, there are some things you can do:

1. Intentionally find couples who are healthy and begin to connect with them.

2. Fill your time with purpose.

3. Begin to journal or start a list of what you intend to let go of and what you intend to embrace.

4. Above all, speak the Word, eat the Word, pray the Word (see Matthew 6:33).

If your spouse is open to it, pray together daily. If your spouse isn't spiritually motivated, then try to keep the prayer short. Concentrate on the quality of the prayer and not the length of the prayer. Don't force your spouse to pray; you pray until he or she is comfortable enough to pray aloud.

JOINING SELF-REPAIR WITH SPIRITUAL EXAMINATION

THE STORY ~
One of my favorite scriptures is Psalm 51:14. I sometimes forget to pray this prayer although, throughout my marriage, I have had to pray it over and over again. I started the journey of counseling, and yes it was helping, but God showed me how many people I needed to forgive, how many memories I

had of people who had wounded me along the way. My mom and dad divorcing seemed to be the right thing for them to do, but I was holding them hostage, wondering why I couldn't trust God to heal. Wes had started a family before I met him, and yes, I accepted my beautiful bonus son, but all that came with the joy of having him was unexpected for my eighteen year old self. Needless to say, I had many blended family issues which left me feeling more defeated. I struggled with trying to share my new husband and baby with my new son when I knew nothing about how to share.

There again, I found myself asking God to create in me a clean heart. I meant it yes, but every time a new problem arose, whether it was Wes not having a job when we first got married and me trying to make it work because of pride; or us purchasing a brand new car when we could not even afford to pay our rent; or simply me breaking glass tables and throwing tantrums because he would not go to church with me, I needed to forgive. I cried out many times, "Lord just help me through this time; renew a right spirit within me."

Things began to change when I truly meant the prayer I was praying. I loved my husband and wanted every part of the promises God had for us, so listening to the voice of God caused things to begin to change. The gentleness of the Holy Spirit began to show me the areas in which I chose to be selfish and angry. I had on a coat called, "Do the Right Thing," but it was not in my heart. A heart examination took place and God gave me a heart transplant. I surrendered my ways to God, and this time when the prayer went forth, I meant it. Yes, I am still changing, because continually this prayer lays on my heart and is a part of my life.

The next step in your journey is to recognize that self-repair and spiritual examination must, themselves, become a marriage in your life; they are inseparable. When we as Christians begin to do a spiritual examination of ourselves, the Holy Spirit will definitely lead and guide us into all truth. To go to the next level, we need to ask ourselves:

- In what areas do I need to forgive myself?
- In what areas do I need to be healed?
- Where do I need to be strengthened?
- How is my intimacy with the Lord?
- What am I hiding from the Lord?
- Am I still carrying baggage from my past?
- How healthy am I as a person?
- How is my prayer life?
- Am I comfortable praying out loud?
- Do I feel comfortable praying with my spouse?

In addition to these questions, there are some things you can immediately change or improve in your behavior. You can begin by praying daily for your spouse and your relationship. As when you and your spouse pray together, it is not the length of time that is important, but the consistency of praying for your spouse's needs and seeking God's will for ways you can serve your spouse that will make a difference in their lives. As you pray, look for an opportunity to create a plan. The old adage, "failing to plan is planning to fail" is never truer when it comes to the struggle couples have when they attempt to experience spiritual growth together.

~ Dear Heavenly Father,
Thank You for examining me and showing me the areas I need to change. Thank You for healing broken areas in my life; I realize You are my healer, not my spouse. I pray that my spirit will remain open to continue the healing that I need to be healthy as a person and as the spouse that You have called me to be in my marriage.

In Jesus' Name, Amen

CHAPTER FOUR

Communication

A word fitly spoken is like apples of gold in pictures of silver. Proverbs 25:11

Be not deceived: evil communications corrupt good manners. 1 Corinthians 15:33

Let no corrupt communication proceed out of your mouth, but that which is good to the use of edifying, that it may minister grace unto the hearers. Ephesians 4:29

THE STORY ~

I believe this is one of the hardest concepts of all for many couples, but it is particularly difficult for me and Wes. No matter how many seminars, workshops, or marriage retreats we attend, we never get away from hearing, and I quote, "In order to have a healthy relationship, communication is the key." When it comes to us, as with most couples, we communicate so differently, but it is worse when you are seeking your spouse's approval. There have been many days of frustration where I want an answer right now, but he has to sit, contemplate and process. Many days, I am grateful that he waits to share what's on his mind, but to a person like me who is always looking for a response, it can seem as though he doesn't want to communicate at all.

We struggle in this department over and over again, and when it's good, it's good. But oh my, when it's bad, it takes us both a minute to get our points across; we both have to have the final say. We both want to make sure that we are heard. Now, of course we humbly pride ourselves on having a healthy marriage, but please believe that we have our moments! Have we ever cursed each other out, broken down and cried, or shut completely down? Yes, yes, and yes! We learned very early on in our marriage that because our communication styles are so different, something had to happen. We needed help!

The Five Love Languages, by Dr. Gary Chapman,[1] truly taught us about communicating effectively. We realized that everyone has a language that they speak. Wes and I don't communicate in the same way, so we needed to learn to speak each other's language. As a result of our study, we can honestly say that we communicate better. It still gets challenging at times; even while writing this book, it took us so long to get on the same page. Many tears were shed, and me, walking away in disgust rather than sitting down and trying to talk it out, was often my number "strategy." Fortunately, our love for each other and our rule of never going to bed angry, forced us to talk. They forced me to be more vulnerable and to share my heart. I had to realize that Wes doesn't listen to me and automatically hear my heart, so I have to learn how to share in a way that will help him to respond more effectively. So, let's talk about effective communication: communication that means you never stop learning, never stop growing, and never stop revisiting, but discover how to love each other more and more.

~

The most important marriage skill is listening to your partner in a way that leaves them no doubt that you love them. The most common mistake couples make while trying to resolve conflicts is to respond to a situation before they have the full picture. The full picture only comes by listening and truly hearing what your spouse has to say.

Another very important skill that we must practice is empathy. Empathy basically means to walk in perspective. You don't even have to agree with your spouse to understand where he or she is coming from. In their book, *When Bad Things Happen to Good Marriages*, Drs. Les and Leslie Parrot report: "Research has shown that 90 percent of our struggles in marriage would be resolved if we did nothing more than see that problem from our partner's perspective. Empathy is the heart loving."[2]

It is not enough to think you are communicating just because you are talking to each other. You have to know what it means to have effective communication. And you have to understand the roles that listening and empathy play in communication. In a marriage, an effective communicator:

1. Thinks before he/she speaks

2. Chooses the proper time to share thoughts

3. Makes sure he/she is not tearing down his/her spouse with words

4. Is sensitive to the timing and the nature/personality of his/her spouse

Ephesians 4:29 reminds us, "Let no corrupt communication proceed out of your mouth, but that which is good to the use of edifying, that it may minister grace unto the hearers."

Once we have learned how to speak in love, we then have to

make an effort to talk more often. How many times, while visiting a restaurant, have you observed couples deeply engaged in conversation? Not too often. Most times, there are couples sitting quietly eating, on the cell phone or engaging with other technology.

Couples are not taking the time to even pay attention to each other; they listen without really hearing. Many expect their spouse to read their minds, with a casual, "You should know me by now," while taking each other for granted and not saying, "thank you" or "I appreciate you."

Now, people communicate their love in various ways: cards, texts, love letters, gifts, serving and more. We realize that there are many ways to communicate, but you have to understand one another. This understanding can bring so much peace to a marriage. We recommend Dr. Gary Chapman's *Five Love Languages*,[3] for it was in this book that we found the main ingredients in our personal recipe to having a successful marriage, and it certainly has helped us to communicate more fairly when we disagree.

ACTIVITY

Your Love Languages
Read *The Five Love Languages*,[4] Dr. Gary Chapman; take the Love Language test (found in his book). Then complete the chart below, and then discuss it with your spouse.

HUSBAND
My main love language is_____

My lowest-ranked love language is _____

WIFE
My main love language is_____

My lowest-ranked love language is _____

HUSBAND
Based on her love language, I could better meet her needs by:

1. _____

2. _____

3. _____

WIFE
Based on his love language, I could better meet his needs by:

1. _____

2. _____

3. _____

~

ARE YOU READY TO RUMBLE?

These things I have spoken unto you, that in me ye might have peace. In the [marriage] *ye shall have tribulation: but be of good cheer, I have overcome the world.'*
John 16:33

Okay, so it didn't really say "marriage" in John 16:33, but you have experienced firsthand or have at least seen a married couple in disagreement. It is inevitable that two unique people will disagree with each other at some point in their relationship. It is okay to disagree with your spouse; it is not okay not to attempt to resolve the dispute.

We all have our own special gifts and talents, and we all have different personalities and mannerisms. It is because of the different personalities and mannerisms that you chose the person you are with now! They make-up that "something special" that you see when you are with your sweetheart. It is those differences in our spouses that we must learn how to celebrate and not just tolerate. It is those differences that often fill in where you fall short; it is those differences that make you whole as a couple.

The differences with which we are faced in our relationships can be likened to rowing a boat: if both of you rowed on the same side of the boat, it would only travel in a circle, and you wouldn't get anywhere. If, however, you rowed on one side and your spouse rowed on the other side, that boat would straighten up and you could go anywhere you wanted to go. That being said, conflict is coming, so how do we resolve it? The good news is that conflict can be resolved. Taking the necessary steps to investigate the real reason behind the conflict is what can sometimes be challenging.

RESOLVING CONFLICT

THE STORY ~

The concept of choosing your battles is something we had to learn early on in our marriage. We laugh about this (and still get upset at times) but for almost 26 years, I have been tripping over Wesley's shoes. Now, let me explain. I have asked Wes countless times to please put his shoes out of harm's way, which, to me, would be in the closet. It does not matter where he takes them off; somehow, I always trip, fall or stub my toe on shoes that he has left in the middle of the floor. I will reiterate, for almost 26 years! This brings me to share that many times, we fight about the same things over and over again. I get frustrated; he gets frustrated, but there just do not seem to be any changes. What can bring about the change? I'm not sure! Of course, intentionality and wanting to change would seem logical, but guess what? Nope! Not even having the best intentions will change a pattern that does not seem like a big deal to your spouse.

That's when we learned to choose our battles: fight every day about shoes in the middle of the floor, or look down, pick them up and put them in the appropriate place? Yes, I'd rather have peace any day than fight over shoes. I choose sanity. Does it mean that I never fuss? No. It doesn't even mean that I smile and say, "That's okay, Wes; no problem, honey." It just means that I make a choice to see what traps are being set for me daily to upset our marriage. One of the reminders of why choosing our battles is so critical in our relationship is because we witness so many people who choose to live in an unhappy, ugly state over trivial issues.

Take inventory of all of the things that you let ruin your day when you could have just let them go, or revisited them at

another time, in a nonthreatening environment. Wes and I are still practicing this exercise, but it works, and eventually what seemed so huge, ends up not even bothering us. We all have something; what's your pet peeve? Let your spouse off the hook. They want to change, and I believe, in time, they will. I still get on Wesley's nerves about my driving techniques, but he has also learned to choose his battles.
It works!

~

In order to resolve conflict, the first question that should be asked is, "Why?" Why are we even having this argument in the first place? Since all conflicts have a root, what is the root of this conflict? And how do we figure it out so that we can take care of it?

In marital relationships, the most common root of conflict is "offense," and the most insignificant disagreements can turn ugly when "offense" rears its terrible head. Unless it is dealt with, when one partner gets offended, the fireworks begin to fly, the insults start rolling out, and one partner will walk away, hurt. Sometimes we get offended by our spouse, and they are not even aware that they are being offensive!

You must determine why you are even offended and/or hurting in the first place.

• What has caused me to be offended?

• When did the offense first occur?

Take the time to write down some of the things by which you are hurt or offended. Writing those things down can help dig to the root of the matter. The offense could actually stem from some past hurt from a previous relationship, or even from something that happened to you in your childhood. The reality is that harboring pain and resentment of any kind is not only painful to you, but also to those around you.

Ideally, we should come into a marriage as whole and as healthy as possible. And even when there are problems, we should discuss our history with each other before the wedding. Self-examination and wise counsel before and during marriage can relieve hidden offenses and ultimately save the marriage.

STEPS TO RESOLVE CONFLICT

1. *Avoid Selfishness.*

    In order to effectively deal with conflict, you must first suppress your own selfish needs or the desire to gratify yourself with being "right." Ask yourself, "Is it really worth it?" or, "Is it really going to make this world a better place if I challenge this issue?" This doesn't mean that you should shut down and never discuss matters with your spouse, but there is an effective way to communicate your concerns without attacking or using offensive words and/ or body language.

2. *Have Healthy Discussion.*

    Often conflicts can be resolved with discussion that sticks to some simple rules agreed upon by both partners:

    a. Never allow problems to build up; handle them as soon as possible.

    b. Be sure to pray before and after every discussion.

    c. Set boundaries beforehand to keep things from getting out of control.

    d. Whatever position you are taking, take the time to listen without talking and then repeat what you heard, explaining to your spouse what it meant to you.

    e. Wait for a response to those items, and then respond or clarify.

f. Be sure to express yourself and provide clarification a minimum of three different ways until you can see resolution taking place.

g. If the communication is causing more conflict, seek a mediator to help you work through the problem.

3. *Fight Fair.*
Even in the midst of a disagreement, you must make your spouse feel safe to discuss whatever is on his/her mind, as well. That safe place of sharing should always be a two-way street. Choose your words wisely as not to offend or push your spouse's buttons. Try to have a win-win resolution, if at all possible. It doesn't do any good if you win an argument but leave your spouse feeling humiliated while you march off to your victory song, having proven your point. If you don't both come out on top, then you both have failed. You must learn to compromise and to be intentional about your words and decisions.

4. *Choose to Forgive.*
Yes, this is relevant in communication, too. Learning to forgive is huge in every facet of every relationship. It takes humility and love in order to let a conflict rest. 1 Kings 3:16-28 tells us the story of the wisest man in the Bible, King Solomon. He was asked to make a decision about what to do with a baby those two women each claimed as her own. King Solomon ordered the baby to be cut in half, with a half of the baby going to each mother. Naturally, the real mother stepped up and begged for the child's life, even if it meant giving her child to the other mother. King Solomon decided that this woman, who chose life for the baby, was the real mother.

Marriage is not a real "baby," but it certainly should be treated with just as much care and concern. Relationships must be nurtured, loved, fed, encouraged, and mentored. Because two adults are involved, there must be mutual respect and forgiveness. It is normal to want to win a conflict, but there has to be someone who cares enough to keep the marriage healthy and alive, someone who will let the "baby" live.

5. *Choose to Forgive.*
   Yes, you have read correctly. Choose to Forgive is listed twice. Understand that forgiveness is quite possibly the most difficult part of any relationship and perhaps the greatest hurdle we will face in our marriages. It is not enough for couples to agree to forgive, but never to forget. It is human nature for us to remember something that was painful, but God's Word commands us to forgive if we want our Heavenly Father to forgive us.

6. *Forgive Without Punishment.*
   Unforgiveness will drain both partners of all of the vital nutrients that they need to be healthy in a relationship. But once forgiveness has taken place, one partner cannot continue to remind the other of his or her wrongdoing. We should never punish our spouses or withhold love from them. They are our partner and not our enemy. Once we have forgiven, it's over! The Word reminds us:

And when you stand praying, if you hold anything against anyone, forgive them, so that your Father in Heaven may forgive you your sins. Mark 11:25 NLT

Make allowance for each other's faults, and forgive anyone who offends you. Remember, the Lord forgave you, so you must forgive others. Colossians 3:13 NLT

For if ye forgive men their trespasses, your heavenly Father will also forgive you. Matthew 6:14

God has a great plan for all of us. Our marital conflict does not have to keep us from that plan. Remember, unforgiveness and offense are like a cancer that consumes us and spreads to those around us, but the cancer does not have to win! We already have the victory and the power to "rumble" productively and in love; that love is where our true power comes from. Consider these additional scriptures when planning your next "energetic discussion:"

> *Do not let any unwholesome talk come out of your mouths, but only what is helpful for building others up according to their needs, that it may benefit those who listen. Ephesians 4:29 NIV*

> *The tongue of the righteous is choice silver, but the heart of the wicked is of little value. Proverbs 10:20 NIV*

> *Pleasant words are a honey comb, sweet to the soul and healing to the bones. Proverbs 16:24 NIV*

CREATING A SAFE PLACE

Do you avoid bringing up or sharing certain topics or concerns with your spouse because you have a fear of being judged or condemned? Do you feel more comfortable talking with someone else other than your spouse at times? Do you think your spouse can communicate openly to you without holding back or shutting down on you? Do you create a safe environment for your spouse to commune with you?

"There's No Place Like Home"

Your home should be the safest place in the world, a place of security, peace and comfort, the communication between you and your spouse should feel just like home, a home where all of your struggles and secrets can be shared. We don't anticipate that all couples responses will be "yes" but learning how to be that safe place is possible and can happen for you.

Most people would agree that Communication is the universal key to a healthy marriage. In order for your communication to be effective you have to make an environment that will create growth, love and happiness in a marriage. Have you mastered openness with your spouse and created a home where they can feel safe to come and talk to you? Have they done the same for you?

Whatever your answer may be, make sure you are on a road that will lead you to making this exercise a priority! Feeling unsafe in a marriage can be detrimental to any relationship. For many, this will take lots of practice and exercise. If it does not work the first time, pray together and definitely keep trying.

The name of the Lord is a strong tower; the righteous man runs into it and is safe. Proverbs 18:10 ESV

ACTIVITY

ARE WE SAFE?

When your spouse comes to you with a struggle or a concern, what is your normal response?

- Defensive
- Offensive
- Open and receptive
- Immediately shut down

Have I created a safe place for my spouse to share?
❏ Yes ❏ No

QUESTIONS TO HELP YOU START

What areas of discussion do you avoid and why? _____

_____

_____

_____

In which areas do you feel you need support from your spouse?

_____

_____

In which areas do you think your spouse needs your support?

_____

_____

SAFETY AREAS

- Listening with your whole heart
- Becoming a minister of reconciliation
- Learning not to jump to conclusions
- Helping your spouse heal
  (allow them to speak about their struggles)
- Having a desire for truth, even if it hurts
- Responding in love
- Wanting your marriage to be healthy, more than you want revenge
- Confessing your faults to each other
- Restoring each other

Here are some scriptures to help support you in this discussion. Consider them when you are formulating your responses.

Behold, thou desires truth in the inward parts: and in the hidden part thou shalt make me to know wisdom. Psalm 51:6

For we know him that hath said, Vengeance belongeth unto me, I will recompense, saith the Lord. And again, The Lord shall judge his people. Hebrews 10:30

Confess your faults one to another, and pray one for another, that ye may be healed. The effectual fervent prayer of a righteous man availeth much. James 5:16

Live creatively, friends. If someone falls into sin, forgivingly restore him, saving your critical comments for yourself. You might be needing forgiveness before the days out. Stoop down and reach out to those who are oppressed. Share their burdens, and so complete Christ's law. If you think you are too good for that, you are badly deceived. Galatians 6:1-3 MSG

~

As hard as it may be, begin to open up and share what apprehensions or fears you might have when it comes to sharing with your spouse. Never allow there to be a barrier which causes you to feel more comfortable communicating with someone else than you do with your spouse. This will help prevent trouble in your marriage. Create a safe place for your spouse; if you don't have one begin to practice. Ask God to help you to be completely open. Open to hear and to share.

We don't want the word communication be a cliché; let's make sure we talk to one another, spend time alone, discuss dreams, goals, and stress-free topics. Laugh together or even allow technology and social media to take you on a journey full of flirting and spicing up your conversations. Text each other through out the day or even facetime during a break. It may feel unnatural at first if you have not been communicating about anything but your "to do list," but you will catch on, and it will become something you can't live without: the opportunity to truly communicate with your spouse.

~ Dear Heavenly Father,
Thank You for giving me an ear to hear my spouse and the message they are trying to get across to me. Thank You for teaching me how to communicate effectively and use Your words of grace and love when my spouse needs to talk to me. Let my words and actions bring life to my marriage. Teach me how to communicate in a way that they will be able to receive. Let it bless our marriage and bring no harm to us.
In Jesus' Name, Amen

~ CHAPTER FIVE ~

Intimacy

Honor marriage, and guard the sacredness of sexual intimacy between wife and husband. Hebrews 13:3 MSG

Be completely humble and gentle; be patient, bearing with one another in love. Make every effort to keep the unity of the spirit through the bond of peace. Ephesians 4:2-3 NLT

THE STORY ~

I never knew what intimacy was when I was growing up, but I learned the meaning of intimacy in a romantic relationship from Wes. He got me: he truly treated me with respect and put me before himself. He listened, allowed me to share my heart, cared about the things I cared about, embraced all of my sensitivity, respected my values, and loved my family, including all of my siblings. He would travel on the bus in zero below weather to come see me and spend all of his savings on me to show me a good time. These things might have seemed normal to many young people in love, but for me, coming from places of feeling like a nerd, outcast and one who could never measure up, I needed to learn true intimacy, not about sex and the bedroom. I am honored to say that I learned this from my husband.

Wes gives a majority of the credit to his late grandfather, who definitely showed his grandmother true intimacy. Learning how to be married as a young adult fell right in line with growing up spiritually and maturing in Christ. In this time, I also learned intimacy with the Heavenly Father. My life quickly took on a fast pace of children, work and church, and at times, it is still hard to really take the time to get into that intimate place with both Wes and my Heavenly Father, but I do know what it means. I would not trade worship with my Lord and Savior for anything in the world. Feeling intimacy with Him has truly shown me how to have true intimacy with my husband, but I had to seek after it.

Now make no mistake about it: intimacy with your spouse does involve sex, and couples should love and enjoy that special time spent together. Sex was created by God, so we do absolutely believe that the marriage bed is undefiled. Wes and I were so young when we got married; the things we enjoyed at 18 and 20, we still enjoy, now! Our intimacy had to grow, however. We began to talk about what satisfied us and what did not. Sometimes the conversation might have left one of us feeling insecure or a little embarrassed, but the talking made the sex so much better, even 26 years later! We have had to be creative and learn how to make sure we were both satisfied without being selfish. Walking away with a huge smile after our time together has truly been a bonus in our relationship.

~

The word intimacy can be defined in so many ways. Some people think immediately of the bedroom and sex, but we believe that it starts way before you get to the bedroom. By allowing intimacy to lead outside of the bedroom, you will definitely not regret the experience in the bedroom.

Intimacy is taking the time to hear your spouse with your whole heart, so knowing their love desires and the language they speak is critical. Taking the time to bring them emotional and passionate fulfillment is paramount to a quality relationship.

Couples often complain about the lack of intimacy in their relationships, but they have even more difficulty trying to communicate what the problem is. For many, it is embarrassing; one spouse may not feel comfortable talking about it, wanting to avoid having any conversation. But it is healthy to speak about intimacy! To become closer to one another, to embrace and connect in a way that is memorable and lingers throughout the day will cause you to anticipate the next experience.

OUTSIDE OF THE BEDROOM
The lack of intimacy outside of the bedroom can stem from couples not speaking the same love language. From couples who are newlyweds, to people who are void of energy due to small children, to empty nesters who have lost—or forgotten—the thrill of intimacy all together—there is no one "type" of couple experiencing this dilemma.

If making love outside of the bedroom is your number one goal, then when you make it to the bedroom, the intimacy achieved should produce fireworks. Couples should definitely take the time to determine what intimacy means to each other. Determine what real love is to you as an individual and then make sure you share that with your spouse. Never leave your spouse guessing what your intimacy levels and desires are.

ACTIVITY

WHAT AM I LACKING?

You can't be intimate with your spouse if you don't know them, the same way you can't be intimate with God if you don't know Him.

Where do you lack intimacy? _____

_____

Below is a list of areas in which you might have trouble with intimacy. Circle the area(s) where you know you struggle. If your area is not listed, write it in.

- Lack of Communication
- Lack of Trust
- Lack of Help
- Lack of Love
- Lack of Desire
- Lack of Friendship
- Lack of Knowing what my spouse is crying out for
- Lack of Listening
- Lack of Sensitivity
- Lack of Confidence
- Lack of Health
- _____
- _____
- _____

~

SEX DOES NOT GUARANTEE INTIMACY

Just because you have a great sex life does not mean that it will last forever. What happens if someone gets sick and is not able to perform sexually? Then what? There must be more than sex to feel intimacy in your relationship.

Create environments which ensure that you are being intimate with your spouse that have nothing to do with sex. Children sometimes get in the way of intimate moments. Why? Not because they are a burden but because many parents live their lives vicariously through their children, attempting to include them in every part of their lives. Often, the activities consume all of the parents' time, never allowing them time just for themselves. At the end of the day, exhaustion overcomes even a decent conversation.

Children are definitely a priority, but what's more important than the children is to never neglect your spouse. Make sure you have carved out intimate time, even if you are just watching a television show together or having a cup of coffee. Have spontaneous time alone – an unplanned getaway or even a drive. Text messages or phone calls throughout the day will also create more connectedness in your relationship.

Many spouses often complain that they are too tired from work. If that is the case, take the time to ask how you can help relieve their load to afford more time for intimacy. Never assume that the way things started out is the way things will always be. People get bored in relationships when there are never any surprises. Consider these surprises:

Husband: clean the house or pay someone to come in clean

Wife: take the car for an oil change and tune-up

Husband: cook a meal or bring dinner home

Both: come home early – or take an occasional day off
            work

Husband: send flowers to work or have them waiting on the
           doorstep at home.

These are just a few examples of surprises that can help you
develop an environment for intimacy in your relationship.

EMPTY NEST INTIMACY

What happens to our intimacy when the children are gone,
the house is quiet, and a routine is established? This should be
the time of your lives! You have time to travel, embrace one
another, and have all the sex you desire. Many couples aren't
able to enjoy this opportunity because they never practiced
intimacy before this time arrived. They never learned romance
and connection.

If you are an empty nester there is a way to jumpstart your
intimacy: reconnect with each other and start from scratch.
Start dating one another again, and switch your normal
routine. Admittedly, routines are hard to break, but it is not
impossible. You should be at the highest peak in your
relationship because you have more time to spend with each
other. Your spouse at this point should be your best friend,
your confidant, your lover, your prayer partner and all that
God intended for them to be from the very beginning. Don't
worry if it doesn't sound possible; it's never too late to begin
again.

Reinvent the wheel of what your hearts' desires are. They
might have changed. Take the time to start over. It all begins
with talking about it and refreshing your memories of why
you love each other. It starts with being intentional about
making your marriage and intimacy a priority.

~ Dear Heavenly Father,
Thank You for our marriage and for our children. They are gone now and we realize that we made them the number one priority in our relationship. Please show us how to start over; help us to know that You still have a plan for our marriage. We need you now more than ever. Help us to become friends and lovers.

In Jesus' Name, Amen

SPIRITUAL INTIMACY

What does spiritual intimacy have to do with my intimacy with my spouse? Everything. Believe it or not, it is important to seek the Lord about everything. God looks inside our hearts and wants us to yield every member, getting to know Him in a way where we feel safe and intimate with Him, as well. In our quest for this closeness with Him, we have to focus on:

1. Devotion to God: creating a sacred place to meet with the Lord and focus completely on Him, hearing His voice only.

2. Fellowship with God: talking to and communing with Him, causing us to become less distracted. The more we spend time with Him, the more we desire to spend time with Him.

3. The Presence of God: spending time basking in the presence of the Heavenly Father through worship and prayer. When you know what that feels like, you to never want to leave.

You don't want to wake up one day and find that you really never surrendered to the will of God. Many couples don't want to make the commitment together to say yes to God, let alone say yes to each other; however, this time of intimacy with God really can serve to sharpen us as individual couples. So often, couples really feel it's impossible to see change. They feel as if there is no hope. When this hopelessness comes, closing off your heart to your spouse is what you think is happening; in actuality, you are closing your heart to God and your relationship is destroyed with both God and your spouse. Shutting down is not the solution; it's just another barrier you put up, and it won't give you the true intimacy for which you long.

Begin by praying and asking the Lord to forgive you for shutting down and then ask for your heart to be open to experience the true meaning of intimacy: intimacy formed by the Creator that can never be shattered or shaken, intimacy which leaves you wanting to come back for more.

~ Dear Heavenly Father,
Thank You for allowing me to know that the most important intimacy I have is with You. This will allow me to know that I can lean and depend on Your love in every area of my life. Open my heart, Lord, to receive Your love and to learn how to remain in a place of intimacy with You, always.

In Jesus' Name, Amen

SEXUAL INTIMACY
Now that we have conquered many of the interruptions that can bring diversions into our love life and true intimacy, let's take the time to talk about sex. Let's not forget who created the institution of marriage and sex; it was His idea, not ours. Romance also must have been a part of God's idea; otherwise, we would have no need for the book, Song of Solomon, in the Bible. King Solomon was one of the wisest men in the Bible, even when it came to romance.

The Bible gives us the tools it takes to love on our spouse. We might avoid God's word when it comes to love sex and romance, but it is the very thing we should look to first. Our intimacy with the Heavenly Father will definitely show up in our intimacy with our spouses.

Couples avoid talking about the actual act of sex because it makes some uncomfortable; yet, it reveals the heart of the individual's needs and desires. Even though sexual satisfaction or a lack of sexual satisfaction becomes a front-and-center issue in marriage, many couples are not ready to talk about it. It is imperative that couples are naked and transparent when talking about sex, and if that happens literally, so be it.

- What are your heart's desires?
- What turns you on?
- What is it that you love about our intimate time together?

Your vulnerability and transparency with your spouse will allow you to become closer in every area of your life, especially in the bedroom. Even dogs can have sex, but who wants to just "have sex?" Let's have passion, romance and satisfaction guaranteed, or at least an attempt for 100% guarantee. "Wham bam, thank you ma'am's" and "quickies" are nice, but there should be a mutual desire to please your spouse, to have an assurance that both people are walking away with smiles on their faces. There should never be just a one-sided option.

Over the years we have heard the phrase, "I have to go and minister to my spouse." Yes, true intimacy is a way to minister, but true ministry is beneficial to both the giver and the receiver. We should never allow ourselves to become selfish in the bedroom. When was the last time you asked your spouse, "How satisfied are you with our love life?" When have you taken the time to give them exactly what they wanted?

We have heard over and over that men are microwaves and women are slow cookers. This term just means God made us different, and we both need to take the time to see what needs to happen; sometimes things need to be quick, and sometimes we need to take our time to relax and enjoy the beauty of our sex lives.

Talk about it; don't ignore it! Take the time to share your heart at a nonthreatening time. Speak about the details, and if you find that your sex life has become boring and monotonous, the take some time to pray for a way to bring joy and fulfillment in your bedroom.

Solomon gave great advice when he admonished men to:

> *Drink water from your own well—share your love only with your wife. Why spill the water of your springs in public, having sex with just anyone? You should reserve it for yourselves. Don't share it with strangers. Let your wife be a fountain of blessing for you. Rejoice in the wife of your youth. She is a loving doe, a graceful deer. Let her breasts satisfy you always. May you always be captivated by her love. Proverbs 5:15-19 NLT*

When discussing your level of sexual intimacy with your spouse, consider these keys:

1. Never take your spouse for granted.
2. Keep the fire alive and ignited.
3. Try new things.
4. Read Song of Solomon and invite his love letters in to your bedroom.
5. Decide how important foreplay is to both you and your spouse.
6. Don't be afraid to ask and answer questions.
7. Pray for a healthy sex life!

8. Explore new ideas with each other.

9. Leave others out of your conversations about your spouse.

10. Remember, it takes two to have a healthy sex life.

One of the easiest ways to live sexually unfulfilled is to remain silent. Break the silence with your spouse. Choose to live a life in hopes of keeping your spouse totally satisfied. Don't allow yourself to just go through the motions. It is vital to every relationship to be honest and truthful. When you just go through the motions in the intimacy department, dissatisfaction filters into other areas of your life. What happens then? Disconnection notices start to show up in your:

- Emotional Intimacy

- Sexual Intimacy

- Intellectual Intimacy

- Recreational Intimacy

- Spiritual Intimacy

Seeing into your spouse's heart and letting him/her see into yours will create a recipe for love that operates in truth, and give you a desire to do more for them. Always incorporate prayer into all of your intimacy relationships, including your sexual intimacy relationship; it is a gift from God, too!

PRAYER FOR SEXUAL INTIMACY
~ Dear Heavenly Father,
Thank You for allowing me to be all my spouse needs me to be in our sexual relationship. Thank You for healthy sexual intimacy. Please allow me to be naked and speak to my heart's desires. Please allow my spouse to have an open heart to receive as I share my heart. Thank You for our marriage bed being fulfilled.

In Jesus' Name, Amen

ACTIVITY

INTIMACY SURVEY

Every spouse has things they want their partner to know, from the simplest things to things that are a huge deal in intimacy. Take the time to respond to the questions separately and then share your answers with your spouse.

Don't allow the questions to make you think too hard; take the time to give answers that come to your mind first. This is usually the best answer.

WIFE'S INTIMACY SURVEY

1. I want you to know that…

2. I love it when you…

3. It makes me so happy when I see you…

4. Will you please make more time for…

5. My happiest moment in our marriage was when you…

6. I would love for you to create an environment that makes me feel…

7. The one thing I wish you would hear me say is…

8. This special touch lights my fire…

9. I prefer sexual intimacy when…

10. My greatest fantasy with you would be…

11. My idea of a perfect romantic date would include (be specific)…

12. These are a few ideas I have to make our sexual intimacy more exciting…

HUSBAND'S INTIMACY SURVEY

1. I want you to know that…
2. I love it when you…
3. It makes me so happy when I see you…
4. Will you please make more time for…
5. My happiest moment in our marriage was when you…
6. I would love for you to create an environment that makes me feel…
7. The one thing I wish you would hear me say is…
8. This special touch lights my fire…
9. I prefer sexual intimacy when…
10. My greatest fantasy with you would be…
11. My idea of a perfect romantic date would include (be specific)…
12. These are a few ideas I have to make our sexual intimacy more exciting…

OUR COMBINED RECIPE FOR INTIMACY

What does intimacy mean to you? Every couple has their own ideas, but how often do you talk about it? Do you know what your spouse likes and needs?

Now that you have taken and discussed your surveys, create an intimate recipe together. There is no right or wrong recipe for married couples. Only you know what your heart's desire is during intimacy.

Take the time to share your most intimate thoughts and desires with each other which will cook up some Hot Stuff in your bedroom. Don't be afraid to spice it up a bit by being open to something new!

Our Intimacy Recipe

_____
_____
_____
_____
_____
_____
_____
_____
_____ .

_____
_____
_____
_____
_____
_____
_____
_____
_____
_____
_____ .

CHAPTER SIX

Financial Unity

A party gives laughter, wine gives happiness, and money gives everything! Ecclesiastes 10:19 NLT

Trust GOD from the bottom of your heart; don't try to figure out everything on your own. Listen for GOD's voice in everything you do, everywhere you go; he's the one who will keep you on track. Don't assume that you know it all. Run to GOD! Run from evil! Your body will glow with health, your very bones will vibrate with life! Honor GOD with everything you own; give him the first and the best. Your barns will burst, your wine vats will brim over. But don't, dear friend, resent GOD's discipline; don't sulk under his loving correction. It's the child he loves that GOD corrects; a father's delight is behind all this. Proverbs 3:9-12 MSG

THE STORY ~

What a BIG, big, big, struggle in our lives… why can't me and Wes just connect in this area? "It's so hard," I would always say. Well, it's largely because of a mentality that I had: "I wanted what I wanted, when I wanted it, and it's my money, too, and as long as I keep helping and handling everything, you should be good!" Such a warped, carnal thought pattern, I had. In the beginning, we lived in Wesley's grandparents' building that they owned free and clear. We only paid $150 dollars a month for rent, but we could not even pay that on time. Then, we went on to purchase a car which definitely did not fit into our budget; we didn't even have a budget! I bounced many checks in the beginning of our marriage. I had multiple bank accounts close with the misuse and mishandling of funds. I grew up with not a lot of money, but as a hairstylist money came easily—and it went, easily.

We did pay our tithes above and beyond, but we could not even pay our rent. I guess I should say we did not pay our rent because, clearly, the money was there. Wes came from a family of savers; I came from a family of neither savers nor spenders because there was nothing to spend. Needless to say, when I got my hands on some money, I wanted things: clothes, shoes (Hi, my name is Neesha and I am a shoe-a-holic), eating out at restaurants, all of the things in life that would fade away. Wes loved me and we were young and enjoying life, but it soon caught up with us. I eventually caught a handle on things after a scolding from Wesley's grandfather. That helped me to straighten up, momentarily.

We finally decided to purchase some property; Wes wanted a building so we could generate more income, but I told him, "I want a house; why would I live in an apartment building?" Both of us unwise, with absolutely no unity, my wonderful husband gave in to my desires. We purchased a small starter home after rebuilding our credit, and did okay for a while until we purchased a bigger home, and then an even bigger one. Yes God blessed us, but the unity from the very beginning was not there. As I look back over the years, sometimes I think about what would have happened had I listened to my husband who was interested in a proper investment. I wish I would have known how the purchase of a building could have helped us to get further in the long run. Did we seek wise counsel? No, I just knew that I wanted what I wanted, but oh… how much heartache financial unity would have saved us. I am so grateful that we did hit rock bottom and were able to learn how to get on one accord. Does that mean that we don't have challenges from time to time? No, it just means that we are on one accord in our decision making about our money.

We have lived through bankruptcy, something we once prided ourselves in never wanting to do, to losing a home, to resenting tithing after losing everything, to repenting, starting over, and rebuilding our credit. God is faithful and will see you through any obstacle as He did for us. He will also restore everything you had, but you have to be on one accord. Wes and I are grateful for all we have and are still learning. We don't claim to be financial gurus or financial counselors, but we do know that in order to see your finances blessed, you must be on one accord and do it God's way.

~

THE TIE THAT BINDS

Financial unity is one area that can create huge struggles in the marriage. Having attended many conferences and workshops on marriage, one of the main problems couples come across is financial difficulty. We have found in our own personal life that it's not just about struggling with money but about financial unity. Is there financial unity in your marriage?

Our goal in this chapter is to stress to couples the need to be on one accord when it comes to their money. We believe in doing things God's way. In order for your finances to be blessed, you must have unity. Are you on the same page when it comes to money? Do you communicate about where your money is going? Who is the Chief Financial Officer in your marriage? What are your thoughts about debt? What future goals would you like to accomplish next year? In five years? In ten years?

How you were raised has a lot to do with how you handle money when you become an adult. Just like with any other subject, what has been embedded in you will either make you better or worse. Unfortunately, if you did not discuss money and goals before you got married, then more than likely, you have walked into the marriage with different views or ways of handling your finances.

Some challenging thoughts we have heard surrounding financial unity:

- I was raised this way, and this is the way we are going to do it.

- You are a shopper and I am a saver; we will never agree.

- You need to make more money.

- I make more money than you.

- I believe "this" is the right time to invest.

- I have to take care of my mother.

- I think vacations are a waste of money.

- I am used to an extravagant way of living; you are too frugal.

- You need to pay your own bills.

- I definitely will keep a stash.

Do any of these sound familiar? The list goes on and on, but whether or not these fit your particular scenario within your marriage, find out if you are on one accord. If you are, become a mentor to younger married couples and teach them how to be unified.

THE PLAN

What's the plan? Do we have a retirement plan, vacation plan, family plan, college plan, investment plan, and charitable contribution plan? These are areas which always need to be in the forefront of your mind. A refresher course in financial planning to evaluate where you are is always a great idea to ensure that your plan stays intact.

Are you avoiding communication about finances? Why? As we mentioned earlier, if there is a gap in communication, period, it will cause gaps in other areas, especially finances. Never assume that you will get where you want to be, if you never talk about it. The saying "Talk is Cheap" usually means that talking without action means nothing, but let's rethink this statement and view it like this: "Talk IS Cheap," as in, inexpensive! Talking with your spouse will save you much heartache if you begin to become unified with your money! The first step to this unity is to talk about it.

No one wants to argue about money—my money, your money, our money—but don't avoid sharing your thoughts and your heart with your spouse. Avoiding talking about it can lead to disaster. Knowing what page you are on financially is truly half the battle. There is no guarantee that there will or will not be strife or stress when you talk about it and lay all your cards on the table. The sure thing, though, is that when couples unify, it brings about strength in every area in your life, not just finances.

So, what are some of the issues which deter couples from talking about money?

• Stress from the partner

- Control
- Pride
- Secrets
- A lack of faith and/or trust in your spouse
- Merging money
- Spousal abuse of money
- Debt-free living
- Secret stashes
- Lack of a plan
- Tithes
- Praying about your finances

ACTIVITY

What's The Plan?

Write a list of areas you would like to improve upon in communicating about money with your spouse.

_____

_____

_____

_____

_____

What area would you like to improve upon to reach your financial goals as a couple?

_____

_____

_____

_____

Emergency!

In case of emergency, what do you do? Is there an emergency fund? What qualifies as an emergency? Do we agree about the definition of an emergency? Do we have a plan?

_____

_____

_____

_____

_____

These are all questions to which you both should know the answers. This does not mean that you will agree 100%, but discussing these questions will allow you to know where each other stands. Financial emergencies arise in every relationship, but talking about them and developing a plan beforehand is another secure way of having financial unity.

Have you talked about a financial plan for emergencies like…

- Losing a job?
- Loss of Investment?
- Unexpected death in the family?
- Stock Market crashing?
- Major unexpected illnesses?
- College tuition?
- Business bankruptcy?
- Loss of income?

ACTIVITY

FIVE EMERGENCIES LIST

Individually, create a list of five emergencies which would require finances, then exchange your thoughts. See if your lists are the same. See if you agree on assigning each thing on your lists "emergency status."

If you are ambitious, as a couple, try to consolidate the two "five emergencies" lists into only ONE "five emergencies" list and then prioritize the final list.

Husband's Top Five Emergencies List

1. _____
2. _____
3. _____
4. _____
5. _____

Wive's Top Five Emergencies List

1. _____
2. _____
3. _____
4. _____
5. _____

Merged and Prioritized Top Five Emergencies List

1. _____
2. _____

3. _____

4. _____

5. _____

~

GET SOME HELP!
There is wisdom in seeking wise counsel, as we have recommended several times before. Arguing about your finances? Stressed? Seek a mediator. Find a financial planner to assist you in reaching your goals. This person should be able to teach you about budgeting and understanding your money. He/she should be able to give you sound advice on how to take a different approach with your money. But you don't have to stop at professional services; educating yourself is one of the keys to success in finance. Attend seminars, workshops and purchase materials for yourself which will allow you to become familiar with money and your investments. Visit with experts like Dave Ramsey at www.daveramsey.com or Joe Sangl at www.josephsangl.com to familiarize yourself with some of the leading financial practices taught today.

DEDICATE YOUR MONEY TO GOD!
This can be a tricky topic. Most couples who live by faith, believe in giving their first fruits to God. This should not be tricky you might say, but everyone has different views of what "dedicating your money to God" means.

We believe in the biblical way of giving. It truly matters as a Christian believer that you obey the word of God when it comes to giving; however, even if you have different views, the concepts of Seed Time and Harvest is a fact of life. If you don't sow anything, you won't reap anything. How you sow your seeds and what types of seeds you sow will dictate what type of return you will have. Make sure you and your spouse are on the same page when it comes to giving. Take the time to pray over your decisions, and read your Bible, and ask God for revelation on His command to give.

Allow the scriptures below to speak to you regarding your financial status and practices.

But seek ye first the kingdom of God and his righteousness and all these things will be added unto you. Matthew 6:33

And whatsoever ye do, do it heartily, as to the Lord, and not unto men. Colossians 3:23

Will two walk together unless they have agreed? Amos 3:3 CEB

ACTIVITY

ROMANCE WITHOUT FINANCE IS A NUISANCE

A lack of money can kill romance in any relationship. Answer the following questions to find out in which areas you are strong and in which areas you have challenges.

Discuss your responses. Showing your spouse that you care about your future will assist in keeping the spark alive in your love life.

1. What is one of the largest dreams you have for our future?

2. Do you feel open and comfortable talking about finances with me?

3. In what areas do you think I can improve in our finances?

4. Who do you feel makes the major money decisions? Is this alright with you?

5. Do you feel we are on the same page in our finances?

6. How do you feel about tithing or giving?

7. How much money do you think we need for an emergency fund?

8. At what age do we plan to retire?

9. What percentage or dollar amount would you like to save every pay check?

10. How much money would you like to see in our bank accounts?

11. Do you like paying the bills separately or together?

12. How do you view credit cards?

~ Dear Heavenly Father,
Thank You for all of the blessings we have; we realize they all come from You. Thank You for teaching us how to become unified in our finances. Help us to invest wisely. Help us to be wise stewards over what You have blessed us with.

In Jesus' Name, Amen

CHAPTER SEVEN

Investing In Your Marriage

"For I know the plans I have for you," says the LORD. "They are plans for good and not for disaster, to give you a future and a hope." Jeremiah 29:11 NLT

And if one prevail against him, two shall withstand him; and a threefold cord is not quickly broken. Ecclesiastes 4:12

THE STORY ~

One of the things I guess I can kind of say we have mastered in this journey called marriage is investing in our relationship. I will never forget, from the onset of our marriage, the joy I had when Wes and I learned that no matter what was going on in our lives, we had to keep each other first. Most people really think it's the kids you should make first. We were both listening to the radio at the beginning of our marriage, we were probably not even 25 yet, and Dr. James Dobson, the world famous Christian psychologist from Focus on the Family, was speaking a message to us that we will never forget. He talked about how many marriages focus on the children and not each other. Couples make sure their children are involved in every activity, every sport, and that they are on the merry-go-round called "Carpool Mom and Dad." Every parent wants to make sure that their kids are well-rounded and receive all that they can academically, educationally, and recreationally. But here is the deal: we attentively listened to Dr. James Dobson that day and we have followed that principle from the very day we heard it. It was listening to that radio broadcast which confirmed for us that if we get healthy and stay healthy, our children will follow in the same pattern. Children model what they see. Wes and I wanted to make sure we were on one accord and had healthy unity.

Spending time together, going on marriage retreats, having date nights are things we have always done. We are best friends, and we realize that in order to stay that way, we must continue to put God first, of course, but make our relationship with each other a top priority. Life has and still does bring us challenges to throw us off course, but we have chosen to make sure our relationship is first. We value the time and money spent with each other to invest in our marriage because investing in each other when you are on the same page will only bring a great return.

THE BIGGEST INVESTMENT

Couples around the world invest in whatever their hearts desire. Often, people need an "insider's tip" for them to catch on to an investment. Other times, they stumble across some prime information and take advantage of the opportunity. No matter how the information is obtained, people will take a risk and pursue a great sounding investment 99% of the time.

People invest for many reasons, but we believe the main reason is to reap a return, a hope to gain more than what was put in. Bing Dictionary defines "invest," as:

1. To spend money or project to spend money on something in the hope of a future return or benefit.

2. To devote to place power or provide.

3. To put money to use.

When people hear the word, "invest," they can't help but think about money. Immediately what comes to mind is, "How can I reap a return?" That's a great question because the final step to Rebooting your Marriage is to invest in your marriage. We've already talked about financial planning, securing advisors, getting financial help on your own, and the like, but you have to understand that the most important investment you can make, as a couple, is in your marriage covenant.

Taking the time to talk about what that means is one of the first conversations to have. If you are reading this book or investing in the Reboot your Marriage study group, then you have already decided to take the necessary steps to have a healthy and happy marriage. Try the discussion, here. By talking about it, you have already begun to reap a return.

ACTIVITY

MARRIAGE INVESTMENT

In this space, begin creating a list of ideas about what investing in your marriage is all about. Then, discuss how to invest, create or revive dreams and future goals with your spouse. Are your ideas the same? Have they changed? Do NOT be limited to this space; this is your future we are talking about!

Husbands

What does it mean to invest in our marriage?

_____

_____

What are my future dreams and goals for us as a couple?

_____

_____

How do I see us investing in those dreams and goals?

_____

_____

How could we invest more in those dreams and goals?

_____

_____

Wives

What does it mean to invest in our marriage?

_____

_____

What are my future dreams and goals for us as a couple?

_____

_____

How do I see us investing in those dreams and goals?

_____

_____

How could we invest more in those dreams and goals?

_____

_____

~

SURROUNDED BY HEALTHY COUPLES

Let's face it: couples who are constantly surrounded by negative company will eventually see their marriage going in a downward spiral. Who are you surrounded by? This question should always be something you come back too. Are you the healthiest couple in your entire circle? If the answer is yes, then it's time to re-inventory your relationships. It is imperative that you stay around people who are determined to work hard on their marriage, couples after whom you desire to pattern your marriage. Granted, carbon copies are often a turn off because people want to be original. An "original" marriage is a great idea; however, there is definitely a pattern you have to follow in order to get the results you are looking for.

How many times have you purposed in your heart to start

making changes in your life, yet it appears that eventually, the plan falls apart. We often use the adage, "Every great counselor needs a counselor; every great teacher is a great student." No one has arrived, so every marriage needs a great mentoring couple to follow. There is only one way to learn how to be the best and that is to obtain knowledge, coaching and wisdom about the subject you want to excel in: your marriage.

For example, when couples want to invest in money they find a financial expert; when purchasing a dog, they go to a place that breeds the dogs they want to purchase. When couples want to see weight loss, they invest in a weight loss expert or personal trainer. We can go on and on about the different scenarios which lead you in the right direction of your interests, but we have only brought these points to lead you to the matter at hand:

Invest in your marriage!

Unfortunately, marriages in current society, especially in the body of Christ, have taken a back seat. Today, having a healthy marriage is like having an old piece of clothing: we put it on only when there is nothing else to wear, only seeing the value in it when forced to do so. Instead of taking the time to care for it, we throw it around in our thoughts only when the thought benefits us.

Similarly, every now and then, we find some type of value in our spouse, but often we only find happiness when it benefits us. Then we go right back into the same rut of never taking the time to give proper care and appreciation in our marriage. We don't value our spouses as a precious gift. In what ways have you neglected to invest in your marriage?

ACTIVITY

LIVING AND LOVING INTENTIONALLY
Make a list of how you have recently been intentional about your spouse and enhancing your relationship.

I have been intentional about enhancing my relationship with my spouse by...

1. _____

2. _____

3. _____

4. _____

5. _____

6. _____

7. _____

Investing in your marriage is the only way you will survive to be a healthy couple. If you never take the time to learn, listen and love your spouse, you will find yourself unhappy and unfulfilled, which will lead you down the road of a stagnant marriage or even divorce.

The world today has given in to the word divorce and does not take the time to see what marriage needs today. It is no longer a beautiful covenant between God, man and woman; it is nothing more than a leisure legal agreement. "Until death do you part," are mere words, going in one ear and out of the other, while "irreconcilable differences" is one of the leading legal terms used for couples when obtaining a divorce. Imagine if we could change that around and learn how to have "reconcilable investment courses" offered before a couple takes the disastrous turn of separating permanently. Imagine what would happen? How many couples just need an investment course? Marriages across the world would be saved.

We believe there is hope. We believe there is a way to invest in your marriage that can change your lives forever. Is it easy? No! We never said it would be easy, but it is definitely possible: possible if the two people that took the marriage covenant together are willing to do whatever it takes to save their investment. And not only to save it, but to make it grow into something that can spread from generation to generation.

~ Dear Heavenly Father,
Thank you for helping us to see the importance of investing in our marriage. We apologize for having neglected all or part of Your Marriage Covenant and ask for Your guidance to ensure that the only thing that comes before our marriage is You. Thank You for healing our marriage.

In Jesus' name, Amen

CHAPTER EIGHT

S.O.S.

THE STORY ~

We have come to the conclusion that many S.O.S. situations have crept into our lives, but truly, they did not prevail; it was a desire to keep our relationship healthy and vitally strong. Looking back over the past 25 years, our journey has been real and interesting.

Let's review:

- we got pregnant at 18 and 20
- we started life with a blended family
- we both had pain from parents divorcing
- we were estranged from our son for many years
- we suffered from baggage from childhood experiences and unresolved hurt
- we got injured from work-related accidents, therefore not working for long periods of time
- we put children through college with no savings plan
- we lost our home
- we filed for bankruptcy
- we went through the humiliation of starting over

- we worked to rebuild the damaged relationship with our son
- we were frustrated from giving so much and felt like God had abandoned us
- we suffered church hurt
- we refused to tithe
- we faced health challenges
- we experienced credit card debt and overdue bills
- we put busyness first and neglected our family

The list goes on and on, but our love for God and the desire to love each other no matter what prevailed more than the circumstances. The Word of God tells us that we must love each other deeply because that love covers a multitude of sin. (1 Peter 4:8 NLT) Love is the ultimate TRUMP card; God's love will show you how to get back on track. His love has truly covered us.

> *"Keep on asking, and you will receive what you ask for. Keep on seeking, and you will find. Keep on knocking, and the door will be opened to you."*
> *Matthew 7:7-8 NLT*

But how many times do we neglect to ask, seek, and knock? We definitely did it. Often, we figured that we could do it on our own even though God was standing by, waiting on us to just ask Him what we needed to do.

Our challenges may not be the worst you have ever heard, but God gave us grace to love each other no matter what storms came our way. What is your story? You must sit down and talk about it, evaluate it, and then lay it at the feet of Jesus. His love will carry you when you feel you can't make it any further. It's a trust issue: we truly thank God for the laundry list of things we have had to endure, but we also are so thankful to God that He has and is still healing us and causing us to fall more in love now than ever. We realize that storms will blow, but trusting the Captain of our ship causes peace in the midst. Thanks be to God who causes us to triumph. So take inventory of your S.O.S., but know that you are an overcomer. You will win!

> *But thanks [be] to God, who always leads us in triumph in the Christ, and makes manifest the odour of his knowledge through us in every place. 2 Corinthians 2:14 DBT*

WHERE IS YOUR MARRIAGE?

S.O.S. has been an international, standard distress signal since the early 1900's. That's convenient for the rest of the world, but in our marriages, what do we do when we find ourselves in an S.O.S. situation? When we've rebooted and it didn't work, or we haven't yet rebooted and we're in a trouble situation? Or when we have no idea what to do?

The scriptures tell us in Hebrews 11:6 that "Without faith it is impossible to please God." We are also reminded in Matthew 19:26 that, "…With God, all things are possible." Even in S.O.S. situations, we have seen these scriptures at work too many times to count. As a marriage ministry, we have been graced to minister to couples from all walks of life. The question we often use to help evaluate is

• "Where is your marriage?"

We have broken it down into two commonly encountered scenarios: Help, Please and 911 Emergency.

HELP, PLEASE...

In your marriage, are you noticing:

- minor arguing?

- irritability?

- a lack of laughter?

- a low sex drive?

- boredom?

- lack of concern for your personal physique?

In this scenario, couples have generally reached a rough patch. They have become too familiar with each other. They are usually too busy and need to slow down and be reminded of their love and the reason they like each other. Many times when couples start to show these minor signs of frustrations in their marriage, it can go one of two ways:

1. They have a wake-up call and they both agree to take the time to invest in each other.

or

2. They just keep letting the minor problems build until they turn into a bigger problem.

All is not lost, however; in this situation, the solution requires some basic interventions:

1. Take the time to pray together and ask someone whom you both respect to pray for you and hold you accountable for getting some help.

2. Make sure you both get involved in a marriage group or marriage workshops, and begin to slow down and spend more time with each other.

3. Decrease the busyness, whether it is due to a job, children, church or hobbies, because those items can all be distractions in a marriage.

Finding out what stage your marriage is in will give you clear signs how important and urgent your investments have to be.

The next scenario is a bit more grave:

911 EMERGENCY
In your marriage, are you noticing that you are:

• Angry with each other most of the time?

• Going to bed angry?

• Having separate agendas?

• Being influenced by negative company?

• Complaining and murmuring?

• Irritable with each other?

• Going days without speaking?

• Cohabitating and growing apart?

In the 911 scenario, you will drown without help. And not just any help, but help that will make you whole. You will have to work to save the life of your marriage.

Think of it this way: if your spouse was in critical condition physically, and the doctors called the family in to let you know that your spouse may not make it, they would put your spouse in the Intensive Care Unit. This is where doctors want the patient to have limited interaction with people, lots of rest and monitored medication and consultations in hopes that the failing health will turn around.

If you realize that your marriage is in a critical condition after having read this book, then it's time to take another faith-based approach for the health and life of your union. It is time to seek out wise counsel for a healed and restored marriage. Can this happen? Can a marriage in disrepair be restored? It absolutely can! God has give people healing strategies and necessary steps to go through in order for you to have a marriage that is pleasing to God and to each other.

Counseling. Prayer Groups. Marriage Workshops. Seminars. These are just a few areas where you can start. We recommend that you start today.

Whether you fall under the Help, Please or the 911 Emergency scenario, or are somewhere in between, use the following activity to create a list of ways you will invest in your marriage. Days are sure to come when you will feel overwhelmed, stressed or even bored. On those days, refer back to your list, together. Make a declaration that you will invest in your marriage, no matter how uncomfortable it may be. Make sure you and your spouse take the time to see where you need to grow and improve and then, how you have grown and improved!

~ Dear Heavenly Father,
We thank You for the gift of marriage. We ask that You fill our hearts as never before with your love, your grace, your mercy and your peace. Make us receptive to Your Voice and restore ten-fold the love that brought us together. Soften our hearts towards each other as we try to rebuild that which the enemy has attempted to steal. Honor our covenant with You. We love You and want to please you with every area of our lives, including in this union.

In Jesus' name, Amen

ACTIVITY

Marriage Declaration

We, Team _____, decree that our marriage is not dead, but a living, breathing covenant.

We speak life into it right now, in Jesus' name, and we promise to invest in our marriage in the following ways:

1. _____

2. _____

3. _____

4. _____

5. _____

We know that this will not be easy, but we will make it with support, prayer and God's grace because God loves marriage and He honors His covenants with His people.

_____   _____
Signature   Signature

_____   _____
Date   Date

7 Ways To Dump The Junk

Do you have a junk drawer, closet, or room? We havn't met many people who don't have some place where the junk goes. Wherever your junk place is you will usually find things you don't need anymore crowding over the top of more valuable things. We personally have few places where junk is stored; a computer junk drawer, filled with chords and old things that we no longer have use for, and even a junk closet where old computers keyboards and monitors are stored. Why are we saving all this junk?

Sometimes junk just accumulates. So no matter how many times Wes and I have cleaned up in the last 26 years, we have to take the time, at some point, to dump the junk; do an inventory and make sure we are not hoarding things which we don't need. Although we made a decision from the beginning of our marriage how important it was to do all of the things mentioned in this book, junk began to clog up our clear channel of communication, fill up our lives and began to make us shut down.

Dump The Junk! There is always room to de-clutter and get rid of things that are slowing you down. Empty out everything that does not belong in your marriage. Take the principles in the book and apply them over and over again. The word of God is the best way to Dump the Junk for it is in His word that we find life.

So don't turn a deaf ear to these gracious words. If those who ignored earthly warnings didn't get away with it, what will happen to us if we turn our backs on heavenly warnings? His voice that time shook the earth to its foundations; this time—he's told us this quite plainly—he'll also rock the heavens: "One last shaking, from top to bottom, stem to stern." The phrase "one last shaking" means a thorough housecleaning, getting rid of all the historical and religious junk so that the unshakable essentials stand clear and uncluttered. Hebrews 12:25-27 MSG

Thank God that we knew how to pay attention to the signs that we needed a reboot. Even while writing the pages of this book, it became frustrating because we still needed to function in everyday life. Most importantly we needed to make sure that we didn't allow vices and distractions to sneak in and totally unplug us from each other.

Well, thanking God for a message by our brother and sister, Pastors Doug and Shanna Neal that we heard at one of our retreats, we realized that it was time to "facetime." They preached a message about how important it is every day to sit and connect with your spouse. We had been so busy that our facetime became sleep time, fussing time, counseling time, and business time, but never the right time for ourselves. It was definitely time to reboot our marriage.

Yes, we consider ourselves blessed beyond many marriages to be able to smile at each other and still love each other; however, any couple can be deceived into thinking that they don't need to reboot their marriage! We had to take the time to sit down and share what was really going on. We had to do a strength assessment to see if we were on the same page. We looked inside of ourselves to focus on self-repair in order to evaluate our distracting paths and to reflect on the areas in which we had been neglecting each other. Reminded of many of our workshops and of how we encourage couples to pray together, it became evident that we were lacking a spiritual examination. We needed to ask God to intervene on our behalf. We needed Him to help us to see what was in each other's hearts and to not get offended by the changes which were occurring, but to help us to see each other's point of view and strengthen us with His love while we learned how to grow together, again.

Yes, we realized that our communication was clearly off, not only with each other but with our Heavenly Father; going through the motions is never healthy, naturally or spiritually. There has to be a clear heart of taking the time to talk to each other, and to talk to God about each other. Relationships have no future without listening to each other and sharing your heart with each other. Communication was the key.

Even when we shared our heart, we didn't really want to hear some of the disappointments we were experiencing, but it helped our intimacy with each other. It actually made us closer. This reminded us not to take each other for granted. Just assuming we were both "okay" was not okay. Our commitment to keep the intimacy going beyond the bedroom had to take root. A rude awakening, we know. Yet, teaching and encouraging other couples to have a good marriage and giving them tools, but never taking the time for ourselves would ultimately lead to destruction. Thank God it didn't; thank God we began to practice what we preached.

What has happened has been wonderful; it has caused our intimacy to grow: grow with our Lord because of praying together every day, grow with each other because we are determined to remain committed to putting each other first. We hold each other accountable for when we get distracted and too busy. Someone has to hold up a flag and say, "It's time to reboot!"

We are getting rid of the blame game and the "whose fault is it," to begin focusing on the future. Regardless of where it went wrong, we both realized that it was both of our faults.

We can both admit that it has been challenging and has taken sacrifice on both our parts to assure that the other gets what they need out of our covenant relationship, but it's so worth it to invest in our marriage.

We used to laugh together all of the time, and enjoy the friendship God gave us by bringing us together. Well it has returned, not because of a special formula or magic wand, but just because we love each other and have humbled ourselves to want to see each other happy and fulfilled. We responded to the need and did not wait until everything was falling apart. You must have a vision of where you want your marriage to be, and when you see the vision getting blurred, pull out all of the tools and resources you need to REBOOT your marriage. Respond to your spouse's cry; it may not be a literal one, but make sure you are paying attention.

We recall again how the Bible tells us in Matthew 7:24-25 MSG to build our house upon a solid foundation so that it can withstand the storm. The only way to do this is to invest in the home.

The natural home is of brick, mortar and the foundation upon which it is built, but everyone knows a house needs work. A natural home can yield mold or succumb to a falling foundation, but there are many steps you can take before you allow that house to fall.

You can have:

• insurance to make sure you are covered by all of the mishaps that could take place.

• communication about the upgrades which need to be done.

• a plan to redecorate, remodel.

These analogies are used for a natural brick and mortar home, but what about the home of your marriage? How is the upkeep going? Have you invested yet?

Investing in your marriage can become redundant conversation, and can appear quite elementary; however, if this were truly the case, and if it were so simple, why are so many marriages failing today? Everyone has a plan when they first get married, just as we did, but did you make a plan to continue to reboot your marriage? Recharge your battery? Refresh your knowledge? Constantly renew your love and commitment to each other?

This is what we have personally learned in our journey, and we pray that you will commit to rebooting your marriage over and over again, just as you would a computer. Remove all viruses from your life; they may pop up from time to time, but never let them linger. Begin to apply the tools you need and seek out to find the technicians who can give you proper maintenance and instruction for your marriage.

Everyone has a different story and ours is still being told; however, one thing we have learned in 26 years is to constantly seek God first and to never let the marriage grow into something that cannot be repaired. The only way disrepair can take place is if you do not commit to surrendering your marriage to the One who created it in the first place.

Take your marriage back to the Manufacturer, and ask Him to give you a personal reboot. His love for You and His covenant with you will rebuild your marriage. Encourage each other and let your spouse know they are worth the investment.

We both agreed that we were worth it.

~ Happy Rebooting,
Wes and Neesha Stringfellow

Firewall Protection

A firewall is a system designed to prevent unauthorized access to or from a private network. This is also a very important concept in marriage. Here are some important steps you can take to install firewalls and help *Reboot Your Marriage*.

Where do we start?

- Attend marriage conferences, gatherings, workshops, and date nights with other healthy marriages.
- Take part in counseling and reading marriage devotionals together.

How often should I reboot?

- Every day you should pray for a reboot or restart. Never take it for granted that an unforeseen problem has not snuck in. Determine to pray every day for a fresh start and a healthy relationship with your mate.

How do I turn off, restart, and shut down?

- You don't turn off, shut down or dismiss your mate; you only restart.

How do we restart?

- Start each morning with love, affection and prayer.
- Read material which will help you have an amazing marriage.
- Be determined to say, "I'm sorry," even when you are not wrong.
- Confess to your spouse daily that you are striving for a healthy relationship.
- Have an accountability married couple with whom you can have prayer when you are feeling weak and frustrated.
- Vacation together, spending time with one another, laughing together, and just simply being friends.
- Always be open to have forgiveness in your heart.
- Make declarations to be faithful to your spouse.
- Define and remove all distractions.
- Show physical affection every day.

Bibliography

1. Chapman, Gary D. The Five Love Languages: How to Express Heartfelt Commitment to Your Mate. Chicago: Northfield Pub., 1995. Print.

2. Parrott, Les, and Leslie L. Parrott. When Bad Things Happen to Good Marriages: How to Stay Together When Life Pulls You Apart. Grand Rapids, MI: Zondervan, 2001. 91. Print.

3. Chapman, Gary D. The Five Love Languages: How to Express Heartfelt Commitment to Your Mate. Chicago: Northfield Pub., 1995. Print.

4. Ibid.

The Ministry of Heartlife

Over the years, we have been honored to pour into the lives of many couples. We thank them for their kind words of how HeartLife Ministries has impacted their marriages.

HeartLife Ministries has helped our marriage immensely. The state of our union was in a place that looked like it couldn't be resuscitated. HeartLife gave us the necessary skills that are highlighted in God's word.

Dondré & Salli Whitfield

HeartLife Marriage Ministry has been a haven for marriages that want to be upgraded, renewed and strengthened. It has been a place where people are allowed to dig deeper into their marital issues and to find real solutions that reinvigorate the passion in our marriages. The network of people from all over different churches, neighborhoods and communities has afforded divine connections to be made in business, ministry, and even life long friendships. HeartLife has been a blessing to our marriage in these and many other ways.

Douglas & Shanna Neal

HeartLife Ministries is a reliable source of Godly instruction and practical a safe haven. We recommend this ministry to other married couples who may be in need of rebooting their marriage.

Mark & Audrey LaBranche

Marriage can be so much work. No one can see their actions bear fruit in an instant. That is why we are so grateful for HeartLife Ministry, where we have mentorship and wisdom that comes from years of relationships that are God ordained. You can seek out experience and wisdom by the multitudes.

David & Kaytee Crawford

HeartLife Ministry has blessed our marriage in particular through events such as the Couples Weekend Getaway and Couples Game Night, but most importantly through the 6 week Boot Camp classes. It is vital for couples to have a place to go where they can be transparent with one another in love and before God in order to help solve challenges they're facing in their marriage.

During bootcamp, Jeff and I learned something that helped our marriage tremendously and it was learning to speak each other's language, which is key for a successful marriage. I know for a fact God is at the center of HeartLife Marriage Ministry and Wes and Neesha's divine connection to God has allowed them to be wise counsels to many couples. Because of that, this ministry will forever be blessed because it has been a blessing to all of us!

Jeff & Sherri Thomas

HeartLife Ministries lives up to its name: it changes hearts and renews life in relationships. This ministry has left an indelible impression on our marriage and our hearts are filled with anticipation for the next endeavor as Heart Life Ministries is adept at molding marriages into the image of Christ.

Pastor Carl & Lady Yolanda Livingston

I can't thank God enough for Wesley and Neesha and their devotion to the call placed upon them to bring couples together in wise counsel. They have been relentless in the fight to save and build marriages and the family and have created leaders from within. Tarcia and I have been blessed from day one with the knowledge of a praying family behind us and learning each other's love language so we may best love each other and God may receive glory from our marriage.

Geoffrey & Tarcia Leak

HeartLife ministries has been a positive impact in our lives over the years. What a blessing! The real life examples, tools, and counseling has been phenomenal. Whether the Reboot Your Marriage group, annual getaways/retreats, or prayer band conventions, there have always been fundamental take-aways with more to look forward to. This ministry is authentic and intentional in its purpose. We love the transparency of its leaders and examples set as a result. The team is genuine, loves God, and is passionate about the strength and restoration of families and marriages. Whenever there's an opportunity, we tell our family and friends about HLM and what they're missing out on. You guys ROCK!

Andre & Mikayla Richardson

HeartLife Ministry's couples getaway is always a fun, spirit-filled weekend with reality-based workshops that provide us with easy to apply principles! We always leave the weekend refreshed, rejuvenated and on higher level in our marriage.

Louis & Joyce Jolicoeur

We have been forever impacted by HeartLife Ministries. We didn't realize how much our communication was broken until we attended Reboot. Our daughters have even changed their communication towards one another. We definitely encourage all we know to attend anything that HeartLife has. It is well worth the investment.

Myion & Ebony Roberts

HeartLife marriage retreats offer something for EVERYONE! It creates a safe atmosphere to reflect, resolve and refresh for individuals personally and couples collectively.

Sheldon & Stephanie Spicer

HeartLife Marriage ministry has been a blessing to so many people. Neesha and Wesley Stringfellow have given their lives to ministering to others. They ministered in a powerful way at the Pro-Life Pro-Family Coalition conference. They do the annual marriage retreat which has kept many couples out of divorce court. The boot camps as well as one-on-one counseling sessions deal with the nitty-gritty issues related to marriage. They are truly saving our world, one couple at a time.

Drs. Hiram & Joranda Crawford
President of Pro-Life Pro–Family Coalition

HeartLife Ministries has been a blessing to our family. Wes and Neesha have been amazing role models in their willingness to facilitate small groups, offer couple's counseling, and spearhead marriage conferences. The ministry leads a significant number of activities that promote the healthy functioning of families. My spouse and I are blessed by the biblical teaching that we receive and the opportunity to serve others. HeartLife Ministries personifies Proverbs 27:17, truly we have been "sharpened by [our] friends." Wes and Neesha are more than simply mentors in leadership and ministry but truly our brother and sister.

Robert & Evisha Sills

HeartLife ministries has been very instrumental in helping us develop into the husband and wife God has called us to be. This ministry has given us tools to work through pre-existing marital issues. It has acted as a catalyst to encourage us to continue to do the things that are healthy and to discard those things that are unhealthy. Many of the classes that have been offered, have allow us to come clean about who we are first as a person and then second as this person within the marriage. I think out of all the things we have learned, we have learned that love conquers all. We also have learned we must activate the fruit of the spirit within our marriage in order for our marriage to work.

Omar & Delena London

HeartLife Ministries has been the support system to our marriage for over a decade now, and we don't even want to imagine what life would have been like without the wisdom, sincerity and friendship we have received. On several occasions, when our marriage was on the brink of seeming hopelessness, Wes and Neesha were able to share with us spiritual truths paired with natural applications that reminded us why God had divinely placed us together. With their help and our determination, The Lord repaired damage the enemy had inflicted on us for more than 20 years. They even inspired us to begin our own marriage ministry which provides holistic restoration to marriage ministry leaders. HeartLife Ministries is truly God-ordained to help keep marriages healthy, vibrant and strong.

LeoNard & Lorraine Appleton (31 years)
One Flesh Marriage Ministry

"Communication is the key" has become so cliché, but it is so vital to all aspects of a healthy, successful relationship, especially marriage. HeartLife Ministries has truly enriched our marriage and helped open up our lines of communication. We are both leaning how to not get defensive during those tough, honest conversations, but to respond in love and understanding. Thank you, HeartLife!

André & Kara May

HeartLife Marriage ministry is absolutely a life-changing ministry. Wes and Neesha are so loyal and dedicated to God's will and purpose for Marriage. Their transparent, no-nonsense yet loving approach to helping us and other married couples has been the obvious...A Blessing! Thank You. Love you.

Kevin & Tarshwa

Wes & Neesha

Wesley and Neesha Stringfellow are a husband-and-wife team who have been married for 26 years. They are the founders of the HeartLife Marriage Ministry which was birthed over 15 years ago. Wesley and Neesha share a passion for saving marriages and for helping couples build strong marriages and families.

They have a desire to assist couples in overcoming the challenges that adversely affect their marriages, whether the issue is unforgiveness, infidelity, financial recovery, unresolved conflict, or just the stress and pressures of everyday life. Wesley and Neesha and the HeartLife Marriage team work with couples to help them become whole and find freedom and joy in their marriage.

While many marriages struggle with a general loss of closeness and intimacy that can stem from an inability or unwillingness to communicate effectively, HeartLife Marriage Ministry is dedicated to teaching couples how to live a healthy, happy, and fun-filled life in Christ Jesus. To support this vision, the HeartLife Marriage Ministry has hosted a Marriage Getaway for over 10 years, delivering seminars and providing coaching for both engaged and married couples.

Marriage enrichment can be a tool to assist couples in adjusting to one another's differences and understanding God's place in their relationship.

HeartLife Ministries also offers a six-week marriage curriculum called REBOOT YOUR MARRIAGE which allows couples to understand the fundamental principles necessary to have a healthy marriage.

Wesley and Neesha live in southern suburbs of Chicago, Illinois, and they have four children, a daughter-in-love and two grandchildren.

~

For more information about The Stringfellows and other resources, visit:

Feel free to contact them to host a
"REBOOT YOUR MARRIAGE"
retreat, seminar, or small group in your area.

booking@themarriagereboot.com
coaching@themarriagereboot.com

Special Thanks

We would first like to thank our Lord and Savior, Jesus Christ, for without Him none of this would be possible. Thank you for choosing us to be a match that was made in heaven. Thank you, Lord, for placing people in our lives to help us grow and learn about what it truly means to invest in our marriage. We pray that every couple who reads this book will have a Godly, loving and prosperous marriages. We pray that every single, or engaged person will be blessed with the desires of their heart. Lord, we are so grateful to You, and we live only to serve and glorify You!

Our life scriptures:

> *I beseech you therefore, brethren, by the mercies of God, that ye present your bodies a living sacrifice, holy, acceptable unto God, which is your reasonable service. And be not conformed to this world: but be ye transformed by the renewing of your mind, that ye may prove what is that good, and acceptable, and perfect, will of God. Romans 12:1-2*

> *For I know the thoughts that I think toward you, saith the Lord, thoughts of peace, and not of evil, to give you an expected end. Jeremiah 29:11*

We would also like to say a special thank you to those who have invested in our lives. There are too many to name: our parents, grandparents, siblings, aunts, uncles, cousins; we love you dearly. You know that we would name each of you if we could.

To our Pastors, we appreciate all that you have sown into our lives. God has used each of you to bring healing, spiritual growth and development to us; for that, we honor you.

This book would not have been possible without the names below, and we are truly filled with gratitude and love. Thank you for sowing. We love you! Thank you again and again.

Dr. Alice M. Crawford

Janis Stringfellow

Pastors Jerry & Chris McQuay

André & Kara May, Beyond the Pen Editorial Consulting

Joey & Marilyn Alexander, PublishAffordably.com

Pastors John & Kisia Coleman

Ira & Labrina Mcray

Joseph & Danielle Stone

Drs. Hiram & Joranda Crawford

Pastor Adriane Mozelle

Pastor Ray & Adrienne Berryhill

Apostle Marshall & Catherine Davis